GROW

YOUR
SUNDAY SCHOOL
CAN GROW

GUIDELINES
FOR BUILDING
A BETTER
SUNDAY SCHOOL

by Lowell E. Brown
with Bobbie Reed

G/L
REGAL
BOOKS

INTERNATIONAL CENTER
FOR LEARNING
A Division of G/L Publications
Glendale, California, U.S.A.

©Copyright 1974 by G/L Publications. All rights reserved. Printed in U.S.A.

Published by Regal Books Division, G/L Publications, Glendale, California 91209, U.S.A.
Library of Congress Catalog Card No. 74-79564. ISBN 0-8307-0309-8

Scripture quotations unless otherwise noted are from the *New American Standard Bible,*
©The Lockman Foundation, 1971. Used by permission.

TLB, *The Living Bible,* Paraphrased (Wheaton: Tyndale House, Publishers, 1971). Used by
permission.

Production services, all photos by Widman Publications Services, Arleta, CA 91331.
Typography by R S Typographics, North Hollywood, CA 91601.

CONTENTS

WHO ME? AN ADMINISTRATOR?

Yes! If you hold a position of leadership in your Sunday School, with the responsibility to guide, train and coordinate other Sunday School workers, you are an administrator! Maybe you never thought of yourself that way before, because the ultimate responsibility for your Sunday School program may rest with the Pastor. But the Assistant Pastor, Director of Christian Education, General Superintendent, Division Coordinator and Department Leader are each administrators at their own levels!

Administration is one of the spiritual gifts God has given believers in the local church. You may have that gift. If you are an administrator, hopefully you do have that gift. How exciting to become aware that God has equipped you with a unique ability to stimulate, motivate and guide others in His work! You become His instrument of divine working in the lives of others. Take time to consider the gift God has given you, and, as you read this book, experience a new sensitivity to the challenge of coordinating the overall Sunday School program, from whatever level you may be.

Paul explains God's plan for the body of Christ in Ephesians 4:16, "Under his direction the whole body is fitted together perfectly, and each part in its own special way helps the other parts, so that the whole body is healthy and growing and full of love" (TLB).

With good, spiritual administration, the church can become the most powerful, vibrant and growing force on earth. You are part of that exciting experience — you can help make it happen! As the entire body of believers works together, each member exercising his spiritual gifts, the power of the resurrected Christ shines forth into the world with an unmistakable, glowing impact!

The church is not a human institution, dependent for its strength on its numbers. It is a body, called to a special relationship with God. To achieve that relationship, the early church had "ruling elders." In today's church structure, these people would be called teachers, department leaders, division coordinators, general superintendents and directors of Christian education. These "rulers" or "administrators" are not to dictate to the others in the Sunday School. (See Mark 10:42,43.) Therefore, your authority as an administrator is based on your gift and on your spiritual example to others. Your primary responsibility is to teach, to guide and to coordinate the work of those people assigned to you.

The challenge is great! The responsibility *tremendous*. But keep in mind that since you have the gift God will enable you to use it effectively in His service. In giving you the gift, "the Spirit of the Lord will be upon you, for He hath anointed you." You can do it! Praise His name!

WHY SUNDAY SCHOOL?

CAN YOU:
1. *Name three common objectives of a Sunday School?*
2. *Explain the difference between outreach and evangelism?*
3. *Describe the need for fellowship in a Sunday School?*
After reading chapter 1, you can.

For over seventy years, the prophets of gloom have been reading the obituary of the Sunday School. "It's a vestige of the past!" "It's a dead institution." Yet in many places Sunday Schools are stronger than ever and experiencing tremendous growth. What *has* died are the outmoded programs and emphases. It appears that the growing Sunday Schools have determined their priorities and cleared the decks of programs and methods which did not help them reach their goals.

One of the top priorities in the Christian community today is to understand and experience the biblical truth that God calls every Christian to be a minister. (See 2 Cor. 5:17-20.) But most of us are not really prepared to be everyday ministers of the gospel. And that's where the Sunday School comes in. Just as seminaries train clergy to fulfill their responsibilities in the church, the Sunday School is a "seminary" where every Christian can be trained and equipped for his own personal ministry.

The apostle Paul describes the Church as the body of Christ with every Christian a member of that body. (See 1 Cor. 12 and Eph. 4:1-16.) This spiritual body operates a lot like our physical bodies. Each part of the physical body has a specific responsibility to perform that contributes to the proper functioning of the whole body. If any part of the body fails to do its job, the whole body suffers.

Just as God has given the parts of our physical bodies specific jobs, He has also given every Christian special gifts to contribute to the proper working of the body of Christ. Paul calls these special abilities "spiritual gifts" (1 Cor. 12:1). No one is left out, and no one can do anyone else's job.

Ray C. Stedman says, "Whenever anyone, by faith in Jesus Christ, passed from the kingdom and power of Satan into the kingdom of God's love, he was immediately taught that the Holy Spirit of God had not only imparted to him the life of Jesus Christ, but had also equipped him with a spiritual gift or gifts which he was then responsible to discover and exercise. The apostle Peter writes to certain Christians (1 Pet. 4:10) and says, 'As each has received a gift, employ it for one another, as good stewards of God's varied grace.' Again, in 1 Corinthians 12:7 Paul writes 'To each is given the manifestation of the Spirit for the common good.' It is very significant that in each place where the gifts of the Spirit are described in Scripture the emphasis is placed upon the fact that each Christian has at least one."

How exciting! God not only calls us to minister and to serve others, but He guarantees our success by giving us just the right spiritual ability to complete the particular job He expects us to do.

Knowing that we have these spiritual gifts is fantastic, but it isn't enough. Sometimes we need help and encouragement to discover just what our gift is and how it works. We also need training in how to exercise our gifts and opportunities to minister through these special abilities. Those gifted to teach need to study the Bible and learn how to teach others. Those with the gift of helps need practical ways to reach out and help others. Those with the gift of wisdom need to know how to share this wisdom with other members of the body of Christ.

Every Christian needs to develop his gifts and ministry.

And what better opportunity is there to develop and use his gifts than through the Sunday School? Through the Sunday School program the members of Christ's body can help one another learn the truths of God's Word. Through the Sunday School, members of the body can experience real caring fellowship as they minister to one another. Through the Sunday School members of the body can join together to reach out to unbelievers and share the gospel of Jesus Christ.

CHECKPOINT: *The first step you must take as an administrator is to make sure you know the purpose and objectives of your Sunday School. If you don't know what you're seeking to accomplish, no one else will either. The Sunday School should be given certain functions and objectives in order to avoid overlap in the purposes of the various other church programs.*

Before you continue, answer these questions:

1. What program objectives has your church assigned to your Sunday School?

2. By what steps are you going to meet these objectives?

There are no "pat" or "right" answers. Each church should develop program objectives for its Sunday School which reflect the specific needs of its members and its community.

THREE TESTED AND WORKABLE OBJECTIVES

The phrase "If you don't know where you're going, any road will get you there" is an apt description of the need for objectives. Planning and setting objectives take time and effort. But, is it really worth it? Why do we need objectives anyway? Why can't we just do what seems right from week to week and hope for the best?

Suppose you're gardening, and one day tomato plants start coming up. Tomatoes are great, but they're not so great if you wanted string beans. So, if you know ahead of time that you want to grow string beans, you can buy the right kind of seeds, plant at the right time of year and build lattices for your beans to grow on. But you can never plant just any kind of seed and expect to get string beans. You must determine before you go to the seed

SET CLEAR OBJECTIVES

OUR GOALS FOR THIS QUARTER!
1. ENROLL 15 NEW STUDENTS
2. 50% OF TEACHERS IN TRAINING CLASSES
3. REMODEL WEST WING OF CHRISTIAN EDUCATION BUILDING

LAST QUARTER WE...
1/ ENROLLED 17 NEW STUDENTS
2/ BEGAN TRAINING CLASSES WITH 43% OF THE TEACHERS ATTENDING
3/ BEGAN REMODELING 4 NEW CLASS IN WEST WING

EXAMINE RESULTS

store what kind of seed to buy in order to get the crop you want.

In Sunday School too, it's important for you to be able to examine your results and determine whether they are really the results you wanted. But in order to measure results effectively, you must determine ahead of time what results you want to achieve. Only then can you design your organization and methods to help you reach those objectives. Later you can evaluate your results, and if you haven't achieved what you wanted, you can modify your methods and try again. Or you may want to vary your methods simply to improve your results.

Here are three program objectives which have been tested and proved workable in many churches for building members in personal ministry:

1. Outreach and evangelism
2. Education
3. Fellowship

OUTREACH AND EVANGELISM

Most churches are ghettos — walled-up memberships with restricted activities. The world coexists daily with the church without the least bit of curiosity as to why the church really exists. It is not enough just to welcome the outside world *if* they want to come in and see what goes on inside our walls. We must make plans to reach out to the world.

Outreach is making friends with unbelievers for the purpose of sharing Christ with them. Because this contact between Christians and unbelievers usually takes place through social events, a peer group organization like Sunday School can provide an excellent channel for outreach. Jesus often spent time socially with unbelievers for the purpose of telling them about God, and we must follow His example.

Making friends with those who are not Christians is only the first step. Evangelism takes place when we actually share the gospel of Jesus Christ with these friends. For us to make friends with unbelievers and live a good example for them is not enough. As the Holy Spirit leads us, we must take the step beyond outreach to evangelism. We must actually confront our friends with the living Lord Jesus Christ.

Sunday School is an excellent place for Christians to learn how to present the gospel to unbelievers. Christians can study the basic facts of the gospel and learn how to answer questions which may arise. The teacher can even help them practice with each other to overcome their shyness.

This work of evangelism belongs both to the teacher and the learners. As the learners meet more and more unbelievers and share Christ with them, some of these unbelievers will want to visit or even regularly attend the Sunday School class. The teacher can share the gospel through the lesson as well as on an individual basis. The teacher will likely want to spend some time alone with the unbeliever, to make friends and to discern his need. The teacher can then share the gospel and give the learner an opportunity to ask questions and clarify anything he doesn't understand.

God never intended that the world should have to come inside the church in order to find Christ. Today's behind-closed-doors Christianity has no New Testament basis. The church must take the initiative in reaching out to the world. We need to be out in the world demonstrating the power of the living Christ through day-by-day experience.

EDUCATION

Henrietta Mears once said, "A teacher has not taught until the learner has learned." This truth has great implications for your Sunday School teaching staff. It assumes that a teacher may not be teaching even though the lesson is being covered each week. It says that only when the learner has learned has the teacher really taught.

The purpose of Christian education is to increase a learner's Bible knowledge. But knowledge of the Bible — no matter how complete — is neither sufficient nor effective in itself. Until discovering the truths in God's Word produces changes in the actions and life-style of the learner, Christian education is not effective.

When the word "know" is used in the Bible, it often means experiential knowledge rather than intellectual knowledge. For instance, when the Bible says we "know" Jesus, it means an intimate personal relationship, not intellectual knowledge of facts about Jesus. "And by this we know that we have come to know Him, if we keep His commandments. The one who says, 'I have come to know Him,' and does not keep His commandments, is a liar, and the truth is not in him" (1 John 2:3,4). As these verses indicate, there is always a very strong connection in Christianity between what we know or say and what we do.

In fact, when a Christian increases his knowledge of God's truth, and refuses to respond to it in a practical way, he sins. "To one who knows the right thing to do, and does not do it, to him it is sin" (Jas. 4:17). It is imperative that we as Christian educators seek life changes as well as increased Bible knowledge. We must pray much for our learners and rely daily upon the Holy Spirit to motivate them to change.

Learners are really learning when they begin to evidence definite conduct changes as a result of their study of the Bible. This is true Christian education.

FELLOWSHIP

Biblical fellowship does not mean social events which take place in the Fellowship Hall of your church. "Fellowship" means sharing in a partnership. As members of the body of Christ, we are partners in the life and work of Christ. And we need to share our lives with one another on a personal level. When one member of the body suffers, the other members need to comfort that one. When another rejoices over a special victory, we need to share his happiness. In this way we are all encouraged. To have the kind of sharing and fellowship God wants for us, we must learn to relate to one another on a very personal level.

This kind of sharing happens most often in small groups. That's why Sunday School is an excellent place for real fellowship. If your church or Sunday School classes do not experience this kind of personal fellowship, now is the time to begin. People are usually shy about sharing in this way at first, so it may take time to develop.

We often substitute superficial fellowship of all-church socials and annual get-togethers for the love we should be giving one another. Jesus said, "By this all men will know that you are My disciples, if you have love for one another" (John 13:35). We need to learn to care for one another and to meet one another's needs. Because we tend to be self-centered and non-caring, this kind of fellowship will not automatically happen. Every man has this spiritual problem of selfishness, and merely organizing disciples into small groups will not solve the problem. But once we begin to mature as Christians and want to care for one another, the fellowship of a small group will make it easier for us to be courageous in reaching out.

THE SUNDAY SCHOOL ADMINISTRATOR— WHAT A JOB!

Now that weve talked about training every Sunday School member to be a minister and setting major objectives for the entire Sunday School, who's responsible for making it all happen? The Sunday School administrator, of course. You can't make it happen by yourself, but you must provide the leadership and direction so that everyone working together will make it happen. What a tremendous responsibility God has entrusted to the Sunday School administrator.

Sometimes church members treat administrators as though they are the least important or least spiritual workers in the Sunday School. They think of teachers as the really valuable and gifted workers, and they imagine the administrator is just there for paper work and organization.

But God has called the administrator to work with people, not paper. Through the spiritual gift of administration God gives the special ability to provide leadership and direction for many people. If you have this gift, God will use you to bring order out of confusion as you work with people.

As Sunday School administrator, you are the chief educator. The educational philosophy of your Sunday School begins with you. Part of your job is to study the teaching/learning process and help your teachers discover the best way to teach their learners. As you communicate your educational philosophy to your teachers, you can all work together as a team. The entire Sunday School will reflect the administrator's educational philosophy — or lack of one.

As administrator, you are also responsible to see that your teachers are properly trained and motivated. Sometimes you will even have to expose your teachers to new teaching methods by observing other teachers experienced in these methods. You must be a person who can adapt to needed change and then lead others to accept those changes. You must love your teachers and be able to share with them. Your attitude toward them will greatly influence their adaptability to changes. Just remember — you're working with people!

Being Sunday School administrator is a big job. It takes much time and genuine commitment. It can't be done half-heartedly. As a Christian you are a minister, and you have accepted a job in the administration of the Sunday School as part of your ministry. This job requires a commitment of your life to the lives and needs of others. You cannot lead your teachers to a vital commitment to their teaching ministry unless you have already made a wholehearted commitment to your ministry of administration.

PLAYBACK

1. Name three common objectives of the Sunday School.

2. Explain the difference between outreach and evangelism.

3. Why is fellowship included in a Sunday School class plan?

IT'S YOUR MOVE

1. Match the three Sunday School objectives...

a. Outreach   b. Educate   c. Fellowship

...to each of the following words:

___learning	___equip
___growth	___motivate
___love	___stimulate
___discipleship	___inspiration
___train	___instruction
___systematic teaching	___involvement
___sharing	___truth
___lesson content	

2. Try this! At your next teachers' meeting or Christian education committee meeting, have everyone brainstorm a list of objectives for your Sunday School. Then encourage discussion of those ideas. You may be surprised at what you learn about your fellow Christian educators. Be prepared to share your personal ideas also.

3. Evaluate your Sunday School. Have you selected one or more of the three objectives described in this chapter for your Sunday School? Do you have a plan to reach your chosen objectives? What methods will you use? What specific responsibilities for each method will you assign? Who will be in charge of each responsibility? Who will evaluate your progress?

(a) If you do not yet have a plan, develop one in rough draft form and present it for discussion at your next teachers' meeting.

(b) If you already have a plan, do all the teachers know and understand the plan? Do they follow it? Is it working? Should the plan be updated or improved? Why wait? Do it now!

WHAT IS THE
TEACHING/LEARNING PHILOSOPHY?

CAN YOU:
1. *Describe the teacher's role?*
2. *Describe the learner's role?*
3. *Outline the learning process?*
After reading chapter 2, you can.

Have you ever wondered how to determine if real Bible teaching is taking place in your Sunday School? Perhaps teaching is taking place in your Sunday School faithfully every week. Now you must ask yourself the next question: Is learning taking place?

"But if teaching is taking place, isn't learning taking place too?"

Not necessarily — it depends on your definition of teaching and learning. Some of the Sunday School's most faithful teachers "teach" every Sunday of the year, but their class members never show a single sign of having "learned" what the teacher is teaching.

The true criterion of Christian learning is not just obtaining Bible knowledge, but being able to live and express the teachings of the Bible. Teachers and administrators tend to believe that a teacher has taught and a learner has learned if the lesson has been covered. Not so. We must teach so that change occurs in the life of the learner. This change may be simply the acquisition of new knowledge or it may be in his attitude or his behavior. But some kind of change must be effected before we can say with assurance that the learner has learned.

Far too many teachers teach lessons, not persons. In fact, many teachers prepare a lesson that will be the same regardless of which class members attend that week. The teacher does not prepare the lesson with any particular learners in mind. To be sure they have actually taught, teachers need to be able to identify observable changes in the lives of the learners as a result of the Bible study which has been provided.

HOW CAN WE IMPROVE THE TEACHING QUALITY OF OUR SUNDAY SCHOOL STAFF?

RECOGNIZE THE ROLE OF THE HOLY SPIRIT IN THE TEACHING/LEARNING PROCESS

For teaching to result in genuine life changes, both teachers and learners must give the Holy Spirit His rightful place in the teaching/learning process. We are seeking to teach and to learn spiritual truths, not just intellectual facts. We are also seeking changes in our attitudes and behavior which come only from strong inner motivation. The Holy Spirit is the only Person who can motivate genuine and permanent life changes. "But the Helper, the Holy Spirit, whom the Father will send in My name, He will teach you all things, and bring to your remembrance all that I have said to you" (John 14:26).

Real spiritual growth will take place only when teachers rely on the Holy Spirit for teaching power and learners rely on the Holy Spirit for learning power. Some teachers and learners approach spiritual truth the same way they do history or biology, and the results are neither powerful nor lasting.

As administrators, we need to learn how to rely on the Holy Spirit in order to exercise our own gifts so that we can encourage our teachers to rely on the Holy Spirit for lasting effects in their teaching.

RECOGNIZE GOOD TEACHING PRACTICES

Teachers need to use effective teaching methods and practices to encourage real learning and life change on the part of learners. Results show that learners learn best when they are actively involved in the teaching/learning process. For this reason public schools have shifted their emphasis away from simply achieving rote memory. Today's emphasis is on investigating, experimenting, observing, questioning, problem solving and discussing with other learners.

RECOGNIZE THE CHANGING WORLD OF LEARNERS

The lives of modern learners have been greatly affected by the vast changes in the world of the seventies. Television influences the way learners think and interpret life as it brings into their living rooms on-the-spot coverage of events halfway across the world. Our technological age with its emphasis on change in urban life and industry makes life uncertain. Our society is incredibly mobile. Today's learner may live in several parts of this country or even in several different countries in his lifetime. If we are to make biblical truth applicable in the twentieth century, we must know the kinds of everyday situations with which the learner must deal and how he can relate God's truths to those situations.

CHECKPOINT: *Before you continue, answer these questions:*
 1. What words come to mind as you think of a teacher? What does he do?
 2. What words come to mind as you think of a learner? What does he do?

Through observation, study and testing, Christian educators are learning more about the entire teaching/learning process and how it works. What kinds of factors are involved in learning and whether the learner really learns what he is being taught? How much do teaching methods influence learning? What kinds of results can you expect from different teaching methods?

Both secular and Christian educators who have studied the results of different teaching methods are discovering that a learner learns infinitely better when he is *actively* involved in the teaching/learning process, as opposed to when he is only passively listening.

For example, remember your first biology course where you sat through lecture after lecture on the internal structure of the frog? You listened and you took notes, but all those scientific names just sounded strange. Then finally one day

A "jug" to be filled?   or   **A "plant" to be nurtured?**

the teacher led you to the biology lab where you had to cut open a frog for yourself. The teacher walked quietly around the lab observing first one student and then another. Sometimes he would look over your shoulder or ask you a question or point out something you missed. But he never took over your exploration. He wanted you to experience and discover everything about the inside of a frog for yourself. And do you remember how that one afternoon in the lab with your very own frog had a more lasting effect on you than all the biology lectures put together?

Now let's go back to our Sunday School classes. Hasn't most of our Bible teaching been more like the biology professor's lectures than the afternoon in the lab? Most Sunday School teachers have taught their lesson by "telling the Bible story" while their learners sat and listened. The teacher was active, and the learner was passive.

JESUS THE MASTER TEACHER

Jesus used good teaching practices. He often used lecture, but He varied the length to fit the occasion. He also taught through conversation and through asking questions which made his learners think for themselves. Jesus also gave His disciples, or learners, opportunities to be actively involved in the learning process. He sent out the twelve, two by two, to actually experience teaching and preaching themselves. Later in His ministry He sent out seventy of His learners on a preaching mission.

Even when Jesus performed His miracles, He encouraged participation on the part of His learners. When He fed the 5,000, He asked the disciples to locate the five loaves and two fish and then to pass the food out to the people sitting on the grass. Imagine the impression it made on the disciples to handle the food and see it multiply before their eyes. Jesus not only allowed the disciples to observe Him walking on the water, but He encouraged Peter to experience that miracle for himself. When Jesus turned the water to wine in Cana, He had the servants fill the waterpots for Him. Because they had participated and knew the pots contained only water, the miracle had a greater impact on them. Jesus' learners not only heard about His miracle power — they experienced it for themselves.

CHANGING ROLES

When the learner is actively involved in the teaching/learning process, the roles of both teacher and learner change. Teachers are now realizing that they haven't taught until the learner has learned. They are asking questions like "What is the learner doing during the teaching process?" "What will he be able to do at the end of our study?" "What life changes show that he is really learning?" "How can I lead my learner into his own personal discovery of God's truth?"

Today's educators know that a learner learns in direct relationship to how much he experiences himself, like the student in the biology lab. So, both the teacher and the learner are active now. The teacher is active as one who guides, stimulates and cares. The learner is active as one who listens, explores, discovers, appropriates and assumes responsibility.

As administrator, you will need to help your teachers and learners feel comfortable with their roles as *guides* and *motivators* of learners. You will need to understand carefully each step of the teaching/learning process.

TEACHER AS TELLER

Area of most
learning activity

✕ Teacher
inside—active

Pupils on perimeter—
passive

TEACHER AS GUIDE

Teacher guiding pupils
in effective learning
activity

✕

NEW ROLE—THE TEACHER

ONE WHO GUIDES

Relying on the indwelling Holy Spirit as the source of all spiritual teaching, the Sunday School teacher guides his learners into stimulating learning experiences. First he must consider the individuals in his class and their needs. Then he sets learning goals for the class and plans classroom experiences to help the learners reach the goals. During the class sessions the teacher guides the learners with much individual attention to discover new truths for themselves.

In teaching which involves the learner, the teacher is like a mountain-climbing guide. All the climbers have the same goal — to reach the mountain peak. The guide plans the journey and finds the best routes for climbing. The group then follows the guide's directions. Some members of the group may climb well, while others are slowed by the difficulty of the climb or by lack of skill. For the slower members, the guide points out an easier alternate route. For the skilled members, the guide may point out difficult areas and allow those members to find their own solutions in order to improve their skills. A good guide will plan as many alternate routes as it takes for every member in the group to reach the mountain peak. During the climb the members must stay in sight of each other, but they may explore slightly different paths.

A good teacher guides his Sunday School class in the same way. He selects an aim for the class session — something which every member can know, feel or do by the end of the session. Then he decides which learning activities will best help the learners reach the goal. Some of the skilled learners will reach the aim with no difficulty. For those who are slower, the teacher plans an alternate set of learning experiences. The teacher should use as many learning experiences as it requires to help every learner reach the session aim.

Instead of guiding and allowing the learners to climb for themselves, some teachers tie their "mountain climbers" together, blindfold them and then try to drag them all up the same path. With this method the group rarely reaches the peak, and none of them develop their own climbing skills. The teacher who uses this method usually fears that some learners will get lost or fall if he allows them any freedom.

Sometimes a teacher will have to see a participation class in action before he realizes how much more a learner learns when he is free to climb on his own, with the teacher there to point him in the right direction. He will also see how a good guide keeps alert and prevents learners from wandering or falling just by giving direction.

When the teacher decides that it is better to be a guide, he may find it very difficult at first to make the transition from one who tells to one who guides. Most teachers use the teaching methods that were used by their own teachers, so we continue to perpetuate passive learning practices.

Many have never experienced for themselves a teacher's role as a guide in a classroom learning session. Your role of administrator is especially important at this point. If your teachers have never observed or been involved in teaching which allows extensive involvement of the learner, you will have to provide opportunities for them to learn this method. You will have to be the mountain-climbing guide for your Sunday School teachers. Expose them to this kind of teaching and give them opportunities to practice with each other until they feel confident with this method. Then they will be ready to try it out in their classes. Their success will depend largely on how well you have prepared them.

ONE WHO STIMULATES

To become a good guide, a teacher must stimulate his learners and make learning exciting and fun for his class. He must raise questions to which his learners will want to find the answers. He must learn how to guide them into learning this method. He will have to plan stimulating learning activities; how to actively involve the learners in the session; and how to use the classroom environment creatively.

Being able to stimulate a class in learning does not mean the same as having a stimulating personality. A teacher doesn't have to dress fashionably, be proficient in public speaking or have a dynamic personality in order to stimulate learners to enjoy learning.

Mrs. Smith asked to teach a class of junior high girls,

but many people in her church felt that she was not right for that age group. She had no experience, she used poor grammar, and her clothes were at least ten years behind the styles. But she really wanted to teach. So she agreed to attend a series of training sessions in which she learned to stimulate learners to learn for themselves. Her class grew and was divided, and grew again. This growth and division went on for years in that church because Mrs. Smith had learned the secret of stimulating her learners to enjoy learning.

Making learning exciting means teaching learners to explore and discover truths for themselves. The old adage, "Never tell someone anything he can discover for himself," fits even the Sunday School classroom. But many teachers are afraid to let their learners explore the Word of God for themselves. They fear their learners will make mistakes or draw the wrong conclusions. To avoid this danger, the teacher goes to the Bible, wrestles with the biblical concepts and studies additional research materials. When he has discovered what he thinks is the answer, he returns to the class and tells them his conclusion. This method of teaching denies the New Testament doctrine of the priesthood of every believer to go directly to God and to learn for himself. It also denies the power of the Holy Spirit to lead each learner to the true interpretation of Scripture.

In participation teaching, the learners wrestle with God's truths for themselves. They use many research materials which their guide has brought to the class for them. The teacher guides them by asking stimulating questions and suggesting directions for them to take to find the answers. The teacher must also rely heavily on the Holy Spirit to direct the learners to arrive at His truth for their lives.

ONE WHO CARES

To teach effectively, the teacher must become involved with his learners on a personal level. The most important thing in the teaching process is not what a teacher says but what kind of person he is. Robert F. Mager, a well-known writer in the field of education, says, "Recent research has confirmed the fact that when you teach one thing and model something else, the teaching is less effective than if you practice what you teach."* How true this is in Christian education! Jesus and Paul each emphasized the importance of a teacher being a living example of his teaching. Jesus said, "A pupil is not above his teacher; but everyone, after he has been fully trained, will be like his teacher" (Luke 6:40). Paul said he and his fellow workers lived as they did "in order to offer ourselves as a model for you, that you might follow our example" (2 Thess. 3:9). He also said, "Be imitators of me, just as I also am of Christ" (1 Cor. 11:1).

The teacher makes a commitment to the lives of his learners. It is a commitment to be an example as well as a communicator of God's truth. Babies learn by imitation, and they imitate the people they spend the most time with — usually their parents. The same thing is true of spiritual babies. They imitate their spiritual elders. The best teacher is one who does not limit his time with learners to class time, for they need opportunities to observe and then imitate his example in everyday situations. If the teacher wants his learners' lives to make an impact on their world of school, business, home, whatever, the teacher must ask himself what kind of impact he is making in his world of everyday opportunities and responsibilities. The teacher cannot ask nor expect his learners to live beyond what he is committed to himself. Furthermore, as teacher and learners together face their struggles in faith and mutual dependency upon Jesus Christ, their love for each other will grow.

When a teacher really cares for his learners, he will be their friend and arrange to spend time with them. He will be available to his learners, not just on Sunday but also during the week.

Jesus modeled the life-style and goals He taught. He had dinner at Matthew's house and at Zacchaeus' house and with the tax collectors' sinner friends. When Peter's mother-in-law was ill Jesus visited in the home. He frequently accepted hospitality in the homes of Mary and Martha and of Lazarus. He went with His disciples to be where they were. He also took them with Him as He was going from place to place. They spent time with Him

---

*Robert F. Mager, *Developing Attitude Toward Learning* (Palo Alto, Fearon, 1968) p. 63.

when He was teaching the multitudes and also when He withdrew alone to pray. They were with Him when He was transfigured and also when His spirit was distressed in Gethsemane. They learned from being with Him and observing His behavior in the good times and the bad times.

Jesus' disciples knew that Jesus was not just teaching them truth or training them for ministry. They knew that they were His personal friends and that He truly loved each one of them. Jesus said to them, "I have called you friends, for all things that I have heard from My Father I have made known to you" (John 15:15). Jesus considered His learners His friends, and our Sunday School teachers need to follow His example.

CHANGING ROLES

The Sunday School administrator needs to be aware of the learner's role in the learning process. In order to understand how to move the learner from just knowing what the Bible says to acting upon its teaching, notice carefully these steps in the learning process.

THE LEARNER'S ROLE

ONE WHO RECEIVES

In this first step of learning, the learner receives instructions for his learning activity. During this time the teacher sets the tone for the entire teaching session. He is preparing the learner to participate in the exploration to follow. He is motivating the learner to explore truth for himself. The learner begins to get a feeling for what he and those learning with him will be doing during the class session. Throughout this experience the teacher depends on the Holy Spirit to make real learning take place according to the individual needs of the learners.

ONE WHO EXPLORES

The learner needs opportunities to do some of his own investigation on the subject the class is studying. He may examine a passage of Scripture for himself. He may use research materials to study the meanings of words or the cultural background of a passage. He may express his own questions based on the Scripture being studied.

The most important factor in this investigative step is the learner's exploring for himself, and his learning to rely on the Holy Spirit for guidance in studying the Scripture.

ONE WHO DISCOVERS

As the teacher guides, the learner explores until he discovers the meaning of the passage or the answer to the problem. He may explore alone or with a few others. The important part is that he be allowed to participate in discovering a new idea or truth himself.

One third-grade boy had been working on an assignment for several minutes when suddenly he jumped up and yelled excitedly, "I've got it! I've got it!" He had figured out something he had not known before, and he was excited about it. It was his own personal discovery, just as if no one else had ever found it before. A truth becomes truly personal when the learner has discovered it by exploring on his own. Through these learning experiences the learner recognizes that the Scripture can be understood through the enabling power of the Holy Spirit.

ONE WHO APPROPRIATES

Once the learner has discovered a truth for himself, the next step is for the teacher to guide him in making that truth applicable to his own life. Learners may get so caught up in the learning activities and their personal exploration that they may not even consider how the new truth will affect their personal lives. To produce changed lives through his teaching, the teacher must help the learner to see how the truth he has just discovered applies in his life.

ONE WHO ASSUMES RESPONSIBILITY

A learner is assuming responsibility for the truth he has discovered when he begins to act on it and make specific life changes as a result of his discovery. Just because a learner explores for himself, discovers previously unknown truth and even sees the personal implication of it does not insure he will do anything about it.

To change life patterns is difficult and sometimes painful, and we often resist even when we know our old way is wrong. When a learner rejects change, a good teacher starts the learning process over again and prays for the Holy Spirit to intervene in the learner's life. Learning has not really occurred until the learner demonstrates he has changed his thinking, attitude or actions to conform to the truth he has discovered. As a guide, the teacher may help the learner plan what steps he will take to initiate needed change. The teacher may provide the opportunity for the learner to take those steps, but the learner himself takes the action and assumes the final responsibility for learning. Through these life changes the learner becomes conformed to the image of Christ.

NO SHORTCUTS

There are no shortcuts to genuine learning. The teacher must guide, stimulate and care. The learner must receive, explore, discover, appropriate and assume responsibility.

THE LEARNING PROCESS

An administrator must have a complete understanding of this learning process so that he can encourage both teachers and learners in the right direction. It is the job of the administrator to implement a consistent teaching/learning philosophy throughout his Sunday School. As he does so, he will gain the respect of his teachers if they see that he has a thorough understanding of the teaching process.

An administrator must make sure he provides learners with teachers who are good guides and who can stimulate learning. He must provide teachers who are good models and will be friends to their learners. He must train teachers to use effective methods that will result in changed lives. He must encourage teachers to see the role of the Holy Spirit in the teaching process. An administrator needs to ensure that both teaching and learning are taking place in his Sunday School every week. He wants genuine learning to take place as a result of teaching.

As administrator and teachers learn to depend on the Holy Spirit and to assume the new roles of teacher and learner, they can be sure that learners will know the Bible better and their lives will make an impact on the world around them.

PLAYBACK

1. *What three things are involved in the teacher's role?*
2. *What are the five steps in the learning process?*

IT'S YOUR MOVE

1. *Match the following words . . .*

a. *Guides*   b. *Stimulates*   c. *Cares*

. . . to the role of a teacher as a:

___ *communicator*	___ *example*
___ *leader*	___ *friend*
___ *instructor*	___ *confidant*
___ *educator*	___ *director*
___ *speaker*	___ *demonstrator*
___ *lecturer*	___ *facilitator*
___ *imparter of information*	___ *observer*
	___ *helper*

2. *At which step in the learning process do the following things occur?*

(1) Receives   (2) Explores   (3) Discovers
(4) Appropriates   (5) Assumes Responsibility

___*feels*   ___*questions*
___*absorbs*   ___*observes*
___*researches*   ___*hears*
___*practices*   ___*initiates*
___*relates*   ___*rejects*
___*experiences*   ___*studies*
___*chooses*   ___*senses*

3. *How do you measure up? If you're also a teacher, time yourself next Sunday during class. Note how many minutes you spend talking during the session. How much time did you give the learner to read or explore biblical material based on your talking?*

WHAT ARE TEACHING AIMS?

CAN YOU:
1. *State three kinds of teaching aims?*
2. *Explain the need for teaching aims?*
3. *Define the difference between a unit of study and a quarter?*
After reading chapter 3, you can.

Just as administrators need objectives for the entire Sunday School program, teachers also need aims or objectives — not just for the year or the quarter but for every single class session. Many teachers will need the help and encouragement of their administrators to see the importance of setting these aims. It's not enough for teachers to do their best and hope for success.

Imagine that you and your wife or husband are going to a fellowship at your pastor's house, but you've promised to drop off Mike, your 12-year-old, at the library where some of his friends are waiting. You don't know exactly where the library is located, but your son says he knows that it's around Fifth and Central. Well, when you get there, Fifth and Central has a coffee shop and the Courthouse, but no library. Your son says, "Sorry, it must be over on Broadway." When you get to Broadway, the library isn't there either. After two or three more false stops, you're upset. "Mike," you say angrily, "Do you realize we've been going around in circles?"

To arrive at your teaching destination, you must know

what your destination is. If you don't have a clearly defined goal, you will teach in circles.

TEACHING FOR RESULTS

Like our tomato and beans gardening illustration, it's easier to accomplish your desired results when you decide ahead of time what kind of result you want, and then plan the best way to achieve it. "Teaching aims" are simply the teacher's expression of what he hopes the learner will accomplish.

Throughout the years Sunday School teachers have almost always had aims but not the most effective kind. When choosing their teaching aims, most teachers make two major mistakes. They choose objectives which are (1) not specific enough or (2) not learner-centered.

GENERAL VS. SPECIFIC AIMS

Findley B. Edge discusses being specific in his book *Teaching for Results* (Broadman Press, 1956). He observes that most teachers teach in generalities and seldom get around to specifics. In fact, many adult leaders resist teaching about specific problems and individual needs because they consider it to be meddling in the personal lives of others.

Our ultimate aim in teaching the Word of God is to produce lives conformed to the image of Christ. But that stated goal is too general. Therefore it's difficult to determine if we are actually making headway toward our goal each week. How do we, as teachers, get down to the specifics of actually using each class hour to encourage positive life changes?

Keeping in mind the ultimate goal of mature Christian lives, a teacher needs to set specific goals for each class period. What does he hope to have accomplished by the end of the hour? He must select goals which will lead to achieving the final goal. In each class session the teacher must guide the learner through the steps of listening, exploring, discovering, appropriating and assuming responsibility.

For instance, a teacher might decide that his goal for next Sunday is to help his class become more mature Christians. That desire is good, but his teaching aim must be more specific. Suppose Sunday's lesson is based on

Ephesians 6, the armor of the Christian. The teacher might select for his weekly aim "to lead the class to know the meaning of each piece of armor and to lead them to an awareness of their own personal need for that armor." This goal is more specific, and the teacher should be able to determine by the end of the class whether he has actually reached his specific goal for that week. As he reaches this specific goal, he is also leading his class toward the ultimate goal of behavior which is consistent with biblical principles.

LESSON-CENTERED VS. PERSON-CENTERED

Another common error a teacher may make in setting aims is to have as his goal "to cover the information in the lesson." He determines to cover a certain passage of Scripture or a particular lesson in the curriculum materials.

So, to meet this goal the teacher has followed the same format for years. He opened his teacher's manual and told the lesson in story form to his class. Then he shared the conclusion or application provided in the curriculum.

Sometimes the class was moved emotionally. They felt something, and both the class and the teacher believed learning had taken place. But the learners never actually made life changes consistent with the biblical principles the teacher presented, even though they emotionally accepted them as truth.

It's great when a class is emotionally moved by biblical truth; however, the most important question is what did they do about the truth that moved them. Even though the learners in his class never changed their behavior, the teacher was satisfied each week that he taught and the class learned, simply because he reached his aim of covering the printed lesson. A false assumption indeed!

In order to stimulate behavioral change on the part of the learners, a teacher must set learner-centered goals. The main objective must be not how much actual content is covered but what kinds of changes need to take place in the lives of the learners and how to encourage those changes. For example, in teaching a lesson on the Christian's armor in Ephesians 6 the teacher may aim (1) to help the learner realize which pieces of the armor he is lacking in his daily life, and (2) to lead him to desire to put on the whole armor of God. The teacher also may help the learner plan how to put on at least one missing piece of the armor that very week. Then the next week the teacher and the learner can follow up on the aim and discuss what happened in the learner's life during the week as he attempted to assume responsibility for the biblical truth he had discovered.

KINDS OF AIMS

The three kinds of learner-oriented aims which we use are an expression of the three significant levels of learning. These levels can be achieved by learners when the teacher offers effective learning experiences to his students.

The first level is the cognitive level. It is the knowledge or information level. Aims on this level of our learning process are "to know" aims — what we know, understand or recognize — basically factual information. After learners have participated in a series of stimulating learning activities, they will be able "to know" or "to understand" a certain biblical truth. By the end of each session they should "know" something new.

Historically, a Sunday School teacher most often taught at the "to know" level. At this level it is easy to determine if the class understood the truths presented or if they had learned a truth they previously had not known. Much teaching takes place at this level because a teacher's success in this realm is measurable and easily visible.

The second level is the affective. These aims are "to feel" aims. They encompass the way we feel about something, our emotional set or attitude. After a learner has participated in the planned learning activities of a session, he will be able "to feel" a certain response to a given truth. A person's attitude about a subject influences his learning ability. Sometimes a teacher must help a learner change his feeling, his attitude about a subject before the learner can respond to that truth in a way that makes a difference in his life.

Success at this level of teaching is harder to measure than at the cognitive (knowledge) level. So a teacher often just hopes he has succeeded in reaching this affective (feeling attitude) aim. The best test of success at this level is the teacher's personal observation of attitude changes in the lives of the learners. To accomplish this, the teacher needs more than in-class contact with his learners in order to observe their attitude changes.

The third level of learning is the behavioral. Aims at this level are "to do" or "to respond" aims. After working through the learning activities in one session, the learners will be able "to do" something or "to respond" in a practical way to a new truth. The best way for a teacher to verify real change in a learner's actions or responses to God's truths is to observe him in daily situations. It takes time, but it works for the teacher who is willing to give the time.

The greatest reason for our failure to produce dramatic life changes through Sunday School is that our teaching stops short of the third level of learning. Some learners know and understand Scripture, and they even feel good about it, but they never do anything about it. So their lives are not changed by the truth which they learn, and the world is very little influenced by Christians whose lives look just like those of unbelievers.

Administrator, you need to study these three levels of learning and understand them fully so that you can lead your teachers to teach at all three levels. Your teachers may not understand the three different kinds of aims at first, so you will need to be able to explain and to demonstrate the use of cognitive, affective and behavioral aims.

HOW TO SET AIMS

Sunday School curriculum material has always provided written aims, but often these aims have been stated in terms of which points the lesson material should cover. Rarely did these aims refer directly to what the *learner* should do or know as a result of the lesson. But since effective teaching aims are learner-oriented, the teacher must ask the question, "What will the learner be able to know, feel or do after the session?"

Some learner-oriented curriculum lists all three types of aims — to know, to feel and to do — at the beginning of each lesson, so the teacher can plan his lesson to help the learner achieve one or more of these aims. The aims are all listed in the curriculum so the teacher has a choice. He may not accomplish all of them. It may be more effective, depending on the scriptural emphasis of the lesson and the needs of the learners, for the teacher to select only one or two of the aims, rather than to try to accomplish the cognitive, the affective and the behavioral levels of learning in one session. Of course, the teacher must not limit himself to the use of only one of these aims, thereby excluding the others.

In preparing to select or restate his aims, the teacher first reviews the biblical passage for the session. He studies the aims listed in his curriculum material. Are the curriculum aims learner-oriented? Do they express the three levels of learning? Even if he can respond with a "yes" to each question the teacher must realize that learning aims prepared by curriculum writers cannot always be specific enough to exactly meet his learners' needs. However, each teacher must make the suggested aims more specific for his class. He may use the printed aims as a guide, but he should restate them in terms of his own learners.

The teacher should spend some quiet time thinking about each learner in the class and his individual personal needs. It is important for a teacher to get to know his learners well enough to know and understand their specific needs. Then he asks himself what his learners should be able to know, feel or do after a session on the Scripture study. The teacher may ask himself, "What do I want Johnny to *know, feel* or *do* by the end of our next class?" Now his teaching aims are really getting specific enough to produce results.

How to choose teaching aims to meet learners' needs is discussed in detail in the *Ways to Help Them Learn* (Regal Books) series, at each age level.

HOW TO CHOOSE TEACHING METHODS

When a teacher has selected his aims, he is ready to choose his teaching method. Some teachers choose their methods just for the sake of variety. If they haven't used a certain method or activity in a long time, they figure it's time to use it again to add variety. But in gardening if you want string beans, you do certain things which are conducive to growing string beans which you wouldn't do if you were growing tomatoes. You should never select gardening methods or teaching methods at random. The best way to choose which method to use is to determine what methods, techniques or learning activities would best help the learners reach the selected aims.

To decide what teaching methods to use, a teacher needs to understand the relationship between certain kinds of aims and which methods will best help reach those aims. The teacher must keep in mind that the methods are not ends in themselves — they are simply a means to the end. And the end is reaching his session aims.

HOW TO USE TEACHING AIMS

To use teaching aims effectively, you need long-range goals and short-range goals. The more you define what results you want, the more likely you are to do the right thing to achieve those results.

Most curriculum is written for a 13-week period, a quarter. So a teacher needs to set a goal for what he hopes to achieve in his learners' lives in a quarter.

WHAT IS A UNIT?

Since his ultimate goal is for the learner to exhibit changed behavior, the teacher needs to recognize that, beyond knowing about Bible truth, and even after changing attitudes or feelings, the learner's behavior will demonstrate that he has changed. It will take time to guide learners to make specific life changes as a result of their study of Scripture. One week may not be long enough, and thirteen weeks is frequently too long for a learner to remember or act upon the desired behavior change.

One solution to this problem is to group two to five lessons together around a central theme to form a "unit of study." This unit plan allows the teacher to use several lessons to build toward the desired response on the learner's part. The content for the quarter is divided into three to five parts for study. These parts are called units. The teacher can set an overall, general aim for each unit with supporting aims assigned to each session within the unit. The session aims are very specific and are planned to help learners reach one phase of the overall unit goal.

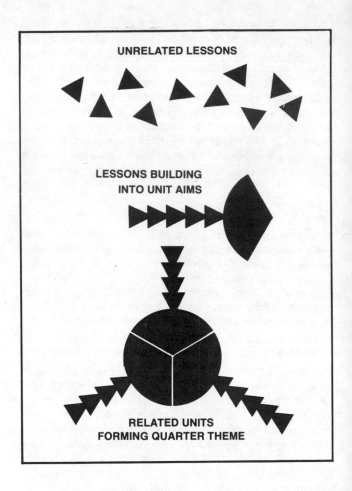

UNRELATED LESSONS

LESSONS BUILDING
INTO UNIT AIMS

RELATED UNITS
FORMING QUARTER THEME

Here is an example of a unit of study for first and second graders. Notice first the unit aim and then the session aims. The subject of study is on obedience to God and is titled "God Teaches and Helps You."

The *GENERAL AIM* for the four lessons in this first unit is that each child should
KNOW that God teaches him what to do and helps him obey;
DESIRE to obey God instead of wanting his own way;
RESPOND by reading and memorizing Bible verses, ask-

ing God to help him obey, putting into practice the Bible truths he learns.

Each lesson aim is a specific step toward accomplishing this general unit aim.

UNIT AIM is developed through				
Bible stories/verses Lesson 1 Lesson 2 Lesson 3 Lesson 4	Music	Bible Learning Activities	Bible Learning Games	

LESSON 1 A Donkey Talks

Aim: That each child should...

KNOW that God told Balaam what to do, but Balaam wanted his own way;

DESIRE to know and do what God says in His Word;

RESPOND by (1) reading or saying Bible verses that tell what God wants him to do; (2) telling times it is hard to obey because he wants his own way; (3) telling or acting out ways he can obey one or more of these commands.

"The LORD our God will we serve, and his voice will we obey." Joshua 24:24 *(KJV)*

LESSON 2 Will You Obey?

Aim: That each child should...

KNOW that the people promised to obey Joshua, the leader God gave them;

DESIRE to show his love for God by obeying his parents, and others God has given him to teach him what to do;

RESPOND by (1) thanking God for parents, teachers and leaders; (2) acting out times they tell him to do something; (3) saying from memory a Bible verse that will help him remember to obey them.

"Children, obey your parents in the Lord; for this is right." Ephesians 6:1 *(KJV)*

LESSON 3 Two Spies Hide Out

Aim: That each child should...

KNOW that two spies did the hard job they were given to do, and God took care of them and helped them;

FEEL that God will help him obey, by giving him courage to do right;

RESPOND by (1) telling times when it is hard to obey; (2) acting out/telling endings to stories about children who need God's help to obey; (3) thanking God for helping them obey Him.

"Be strong and of a good courage; be not afraid." Joshua 1:9

LESSON 4 A River Opens Up!

Aim: That each child should...

KNOW that Joshua and the people obeyed God's command to be courageous, and God showed them His great power;

FEEL that the command and promise in Joshua 1:9 are for him;

RESPOND by (1) saying Joshua 1:9 from memory; (2) telling fears children his age have; (3) asking God to help him obey His command to be strong and of good courage; (4) thanking God for His promise to be with him wherever he goes.

"Be strong and of...good courage; be not afraid...for the LORD your God is with you wherever you go." Joshua 1:9

Notice how each lesson aim supported the general or "unit" aim by being related. Even more so, did you notice how specific they were?

BUILDING UP TO ACTION

The teacher may also emphasize different kinds of aims in different sessions as he builds up to leading the learners to take action. On the first Sunday of a unit he may emphasize the "to feel" aim. The second Sunday he may emphasize the "to know" level. Perhaps the third Sunday will center again on the "to feel" aim to change the learners' attitudes. On the last Sunday the teacher may help learners answer the "So what?" question by focusing on the "to respond" aim. The pattern isn't always the same. The order which the teacher follows for the aims will depend on the Scripture he is teaching and also on the needs of the learners in the class. But all four Sundays should build up to the "to do" aim, the desired life changes.

If your Sunday School teachers are not now using specific and learner-oriented aims, you as administrator can lead them to see the value of setting the right kinds of aims. You also can help them to understand the significance of the three kinds of aims, how to divide a quarter into related units and how to set aims for each session and unit. Most important, you will also want to provide time in your planning meetings for your teachers and department leaders to discuss and choose appropriate aims. Whether your Sunday School leaders and teachers learn how to use aims properly to meet specific needs of their students will depend largely on your leadership. Remember, aims should tell us what the learners should be able to do as a result of their study.

PLAYBACK

1. State three kinds of teaching aims.

2. Explain the need for teaching aims.

3. Define the difference between a unit of study and a quarter.

IT'S YOUR MOVE

1. Circle the words which emphasize the response level of learning.

evaluate	become
understand	sensitive to
check	grasp
sense	compare
draw	share
verify	plan
identify	observe
find	see
look	analyze
discover	summarize
realize	notice
consider	examine
conclude	apply
respond to	list
empathize	investigate
design	illustrate

2. *Look at your present Sunday School curriculum. Is it divided into units of study? Are the aims written out for each quarter, unit and session? Are the session aims specific and the unit aims more general? Are the aims content or learner oriented?*

WHAT ARE THE OBSTACLES TO CHANGE?

CAN YOU:
1. *Identify the five basic obstacles to change in the average Sunday School?*
2. *List the answer to each of the above obstacles?*
After reading chapter 4, you can.

In order to grow, every living organism must experience change. Our physical bodies are changing constantly. New skin and new blood cells are forming as the old ones are dying. If we do not change, we die.

Change also takes place in the area of mental ideas, emotional attitudes and habits — but not as readily as our bodies make biological changes. For mental and emotional change we need adequate motivation and guidance.

What about the Sunday School? Does it need to change? Yes, if it's going to grow. Some Sunday Schools need to change because their ministry is not effective in meeting the needs of the people. Other Sunday Schools need to change because their teaching procedures cause boredom in the learners' attitudes. Some Sunday Schools have grown, and the complexity of size necessitates change in order to better teach larger numbers of people.

To implement a new teaching/learning philosophy with emphasis on learner participation will require many changes in the traditional Sunday School. But if we don't make the changes, we may not produce real results in the lives of our learners. And the Sunday School will die like any other living organism which rejects change.

To help our Sunday Schools grow, we must identify and understand the obstacles to needed change. Then we can begin to overcome these obstacles. The obstacle in your own Sunday School may be people's *fear of change* in any form. It may be a *lack of time and resources.* Or it may be *lack of classroom space, a shortage of skilled leaders or equipment.* The obstacles may be *financial problems.*

OBSTACLES TO CHANGE

The Sunday School leader who is responsible for encouraging and planning and for change is the administrator. And every administrator's obstacles will be slightly different and unique to his own Sunday School. But he must deal with each obstacle or problem individually if he wants successful and lasting change.

CHECKPOINT: *Before you continue, identify the specific obstacles that may be preventing needed changes in your own Sunday School by labeling the blocks in figure 13.*

HOW TO OVERCOME FIVE BASIC PROBLEMS

Every Sunday School has certain obstacles which prevent innovative changes. They hinder teachers from becoming effective guides and learners from assuming responsibility. These obstacles vary in detail from one Sunday School to another, but they can be generally categorized into five basic areas.

1. Rationale for Teaching/Learning Strategy
2. The Sunday School Session Structure
3. The Roles of the Sunday School Leaders
4. The Facilities
5. The Methods of Planning and Training

PROBLEM #1: RATIONALE FOR
TEACHING/LEARNING STRATEGY

The greatest obstacle to change in most churches is the lack of an adequate rationale for change. It is always difficult to get people to change when they are not convinced that the change is needed. If teachers feel the administrator wants to make changes just for the sake of change or just to prove he has the authority to make demands, they will resist strongly. An administrator doesn't get very far when he tries to force changes on his staff. If teachers and department leaders are not given sufficient explanation and encouragement to accept new roles, they will not be motivated to change.

ANSWER: PROVIDE RATIONALE FOR CHANGE

The first step the administrator needs to take is to define his goal and direction. He must think through what he believes about the teaching/learning process. Everything else depends on that foundation. What you believe about teaching/learning affects the entire Sunday School — program, structure, facilities, planning and training. Begin to implement changes by communicating to your staff what you believe about teaching/learning and why some methods are better than others. Ask for their suggestions based on their teaching experience. Help them to see how important learner participation is and how it produces results. (1) Be a model for your teachers. As you teach them, use learner-participation methods and actually teach them as you want them to teach their learners. (2)

Find a class or a department which can be used as a model. As you provide your staff with a rationale for change, they become sympathetic to the changes you want to make.

PROBLEM #2: THE SUNDAY SCHOOL
SESSION STRUCTURE

When you and your leaders have agreed on a teaching/learning process which allows learners to move through the entire learning process from instructional input all the way to assuming responsibility, you must then examine your Sunday School session structure.

A traditional 60-minute session usually has 20 minutes of department time for an opening or closing assembly, 10 minutes of break time for learners to move from the assembly to their classes and 30 minutes of class time. Teaching styles, programs and even curriculum have been designed to accommodate this traditional session structure. This structure produces active teachers and passive learners, because 30 minutes of class time is not enough time for participation learning. Just one involvement activity can take 30 minutes!

What actually happens during the 30 minutes of class time in a traditional Sunday School? The teacher is expected to cover the Bible story content in the teacher's quarterly, and that could take 45-55 minutes. It's impossible to cover all the material, especially if learners interrupt with questions or discussion. Activities may be suggested with each lesson, but there is not enough class time for these activities. With experience a teacher learns to finish telling the lesson just as the bell rings, indicating that it's time for church.

What happens to the learners during this class time? They listen to the lesson, but they are not guided through the steps of the teaching/learning process. So they never reach the point of assuming responsibility for any personal life changes.

We cannot institute changes in the teaching/learning process as long as we maintain this kind of Sunday School structure, no matter how much teachers and leaders may want to change. They simply cannot do participation teaching with only 30 minutes of class time.

ANSWER: REDESIGN THE ENTIRE SUNDAY SCHOOL SESSION TO MEET ONE TEACHING AIM

Many activities which we have traditionally included in opening or closing assemblies become more effective when they take place at a different time. For instance, introducing visitors is more practical in the class situation since getting to know people is easier in small groups. Prayer can also be more personal and meaningful in a small group. The offering can be taken as learners enter the room or while they are moving around between activities during the session. Announcements can be placed on bulletin boards or mimeographed as pass-outs. Inspirational devotionals which are unrelated to the lesson and the teaching aim only take time away from classroom learning activities and experiences.

If you redesign the entire session around one teaching aim, eliminating the opening or closing assembly time, your teachers will have 60 minutes of teaching time. In this longer period the teacher will have time to guide learners through one or more learning experiences. With this kind of Total Session Teaching, whether the learners are involved in a department group or class group activity, everything that occurs during the session relates to the lesson for the day and builds up to reaching one teaching aim. Recommended session structures for each age level are given in the *Ways to Plan and Organize Your Sunday School* (Regal Books) series.

PROBLEM #3: THE ROLES OF THE SUNDAY SCHOOL LEADERS

In the traditional structure the department leader sees his role as working with program instead of with people. Rather than being actively involved with teachers and learners, he plans an inspirational talk or program for the opening or closing assembly. He has very little contact with the actual teaching/learning process. Because the department leader works independently of the teachers as he plans his program, the assembly is therefore unrelated to the classroom lesson. Teachers also work independently as they plan their class time, so that teachers and department leaders are working toward separate goals. The teaching within the department is not coordinated, even when the same lesson is being taught in each class.

ANSWER: REDIRECT THE LEADERS' RESPONSIBILITIES

In order to change our teaching/learning concepts and to redesign the Sunday School session, we must review the leadership roles of both teachers and their supervisors, who are called department superintendents or leaders. In Total Session Teaching the department leader becomes a guide of teachers as teachers are guides of learners. He works closely with all the teachers in his department and becomes actively involved with them and with their learners. He leads the department to function as a real team. He supports and leads the teachers and helps them to become better teachers. The department leader works with the teachers to plan a coordinated session centered around one teaching aim. He may also supervise large-group activities which support the aim of the entire session. His role, which is even more vital now than it was in the traditional structure, is exciting because he becomes involved in the actual teaching process.

PROBLEM #4: THE FACILITIES

Sunday School leaders often make the mistake of allowing their facilities to determine their program. But we must work the other way around — our teaching/learning philosophy and our program should determine the kind of facility we build. Many Sunday School departments contain no resource or reference materials, so teachers assume they must teach without them.

ANSWER: ADAPT THE ROOM ENVIRONMENT

The room environment deserves special attention since it influences the learning process. The teacher or department leader should equip each department room with resource materials, activity supplies and reference books. If your rooms aren't ideally suited for the program you want, go ahead and implement your program choice anyway. Adapt the facility to the program. Think of the building or room as a third partner in teaching — the teacher/the learner/the room.

PROBLEM #5: THE METHODS OF PLANNING AND TRAINING

Most Sunday School planning conferences or retreats are primarily informational or inspirational. During these meetings the teachers and leaders sit and listen to church business or devotional messages. They have little or no opportunity to talk together and make specific plans for future Sunday School sessions. They receive no practical training in new teaching methods.

ANSWER: DEVELOP NEW PLANNING AND
TRAINING METHODS

Even though they are willing to change, many people don't know how. They have a skill problem as well as an attitudinal problem. Because people do what is familiar, you must train your teachers in new teaching methods. Give them opportunities to practice with each other and to experience the feel of these methods for themselves. Your training program must support your teaching/ /learning concept.

Training should not include all the teachers in the entire Sunday School together. The needs of the teachers in the various divisions — Early Childhood, Children, Youth and Adults — vary widely. Plan your training to meet the specific needs of teachers in these different groupings.

In addition to training, teachers need opportunities for specific planning together. To work as a team on Sunday, they need to plan as a team once a week or once a month. The minimum meeting/planning time should be once per unit. The purpose of these meetings is not just for announcing general information to your teachers. These planning meetings should be structured to help your teachers implement the teaching/learning philosophy. It is a time for teachers to plan the lessons in the unit of study.

MANAGING CHANGE

As you overcome these five basic obstacles, you are changing your Sunday School into an effective, growing organism with great potential to change learners' lives and to reach out to unbelievers in the community. Overcoming obstacles and resistance to change isn't impossible. But managing these changes requires love, patience, understanding and tact on the part of the administrator.

Leaders confront tremendous resistance when they hear new ideas, return to their churches and say, "Guess what? Next week we're changing!" Then comes the barrage. The people aren't properly prepared for change, and they resist it every step of the way.

Give your staff good reasons why you want to institute changes. Expose them to the way you want them to go. Allow them to practice with each other. Give them a supportive training program. When they see the kinds of results they can get with participation teaching, they will *want* to make the necessary changes.

PLAYBACK

1. Identify five basic obstacles to change in the Sunday School.

2. List the answers for dealing with each of the above obstacles.

IT'S YOUR MOVE

1. Describe your Sunday School session. How many minutes do you have for Sunday School? How is the total time usually divided? How is the class time spent? What kinds of learner involvement occur?

2. How could you restructure your Sunday School session for better learning? How could you redirect your Sunday School leaders' responsibilities? How would you begin to provide a rationale for change in your Sunday School? How can you rearrange the room environment in your department for better class participation? What would you need to do to develop an effective training/planning program?

HOW TO GROUP FOR LEARNING

CAN YOU:
1. *Name the four basic age divisions in the Sunday School?*
2. *List the correct sizes for classes in each division?*
3. *Give definitions for a class, a department and a division?*
After reading chapter 5, you can.

As you develop your own teaching/learning philosophy, you will discover how much your teaching methods will influence the ways you group learners for learning. You will need to select grouping arrangements which support the kind of teaching you want your teachers to do.

For instance, if you emphasize the lecture method of teaching, your classes can get very large because all the learners are passive. But if you want your teachers to be guides and your learners to be active explorers in the teaching/learning process, then your classes must be smaller to allow for learning activities and personal attention to each learner.

Even Jesus' teaching was influenced by the size of the group of learners He was teaching. He was able to give more individual attention when He taught the twelve disciples than when He taught the great multitudes who followed Him.

Developing a plan for grouping all the different age levels in your Sunday School can be complicated, especially in very large Sunday Schools. You will have to study and plan carefully to determine and implement the best grouping arrangement for your own Sunday School. The charts and diagrams in this chapter will help you find grouping arrangements which will improve your Bible teaching and learning program.

The basic groupings into which you will need to divide your learners are classes, departments and divisions. We must be sure we understand the definitions of these groupings.

1. Class — a group of learners and a teacher with the recommended learner/teacher ratio.

2. Department — two or more classes studying the same lesson. (In some Sunday Schools, classes studying different lessons meet together for an assembly time. This grouping may also be considered a department for organizational purposes.)

3. Division — the term that describes the four broad categories for age grouping in the Sunday School — Early Childhood, Children, Youth, Adult. If your Sunday School has any learners in the proper age ranges, you have a division in that category, regardless of the number of learners.

DIVISIONS

A division is the broadest category in the grouping arrangement. Sunday Schools have traditionally divided ages into categories like nursery, beginner, kindergarten, primary, junior and others. But Christian educators and administrators who recognize the value of teaching which allows for student involvement are reexamining these categories. They recommend dividing the Sunday School into new broader age categories. They have tested and recommended four basic divisions — Early Childhood, Children, Youth and Adult. Here are the age or grade ranges for each division:

DIVISION	AGE	GRADE
Early Childhood	Birth–5 years	
Children		1–6
Youth		7–12
Adult	18–up	

Learners in each of these four divisions have distinctly different needs. As you group into these broad divisions in your Sunday School, you will be better prepared to recognize those needs and to meet them.

CLASSES AND DEPARTMENTS

After recognizing the divisions, you can begin to determine what size your classes and departments need to be. The number of learners which a teacher can teach effectively varies in each division. Here are the recommended maximum number of learners for classes and departments in each division and the teacher/learner ratio:

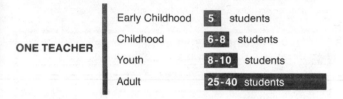

ONE TEACHER

Early Childhood	5	students
Childhood	6-8	students
Youth	8-10	students
Adult	25-40	students

You may need to make some changes in your Sunday School in order to get your classes and departments to the correct size. You may even feel that the teacher ratio in the Early Childhood division of one teacher for every four to six learners is unachievable. But remember that the learner must have the guidance of his teacher if he is going to be an explorer. If classes get too large before they are divided, the teacher may not be able to function as a guide even if he has the desire and skill. You must select grouping arrangements which support the kind of teaching you want your teachers to accomplish.

CHECKPOINT: *How does your Sunday School measure up? Study the charts carefully and see how your Sunday School matches the recommended class and department sizes. An example is provided for Early Childhood, Children, Youth and Adult departments for both large and small Sunday Schools.*

GROUPING THE EARLY CHILDHOOD DIVISION

Other factors besides numerical growth influence grouping in your Sunday School, especially in the Early Childhood division. In this age group you must also consider the number of personnel and the amount of space available. In addition, the numerical increase per age is not always what we expect. For instance, we may have many two-year-olds and only a few five-year-olds. This will influence our decision as to how to divide.

Overcrowded conditions in the Early Childhood room severely limit the instructional program. A word of caution: don't wait until the department gets overcrowded to plan for its division. Instead of classes you should emphasize departments in the Early Childhood division because in the larger grouping teachers can offer a greater variety of learning activities for children to choose from.

GROUPING CHILDREN IN THE EARLY CHILDHOOD DIVISION

...when the attendance numbers less than:

5	30	50	80	110	220
You need 1 department of children...	You need 2 departments of children...	You need 3 departments of children...	You need 5 departments of children...	You need 6 departments of children...	You need 12 departments of children...
			Babies	Babies	Babies
	0-1 years	0-1 years	Toddlers	Toddlers	Toddlers
		2-3 years	2's	2's	2's 2's
0-5 years			3's	3's	3's 3's
	2-5 years			4's	4's 4's
		4-5 years	4-5 years		
				5's	5's 5's
...with 1 department leader and 1 teacher	...with 2 department leaders, 2-5 teachers	...with 3 department leaders, 3-10 teachers	...with 5 department leaders, 5-16 teachers	...with 6 department leaders, 6-22 teachers	...with 12 department leaders, 12-44 teachers

ASSUMPTIONS:
1. There is adequate personnel.
2. There is adequate space.
3. There are approximately the same number of children in each age group.

GROUPING THE CHILDREN'S DIVISION

Sunday Schools which have from twelve to twenty-four children attending in grades one through six will probably have two to three classes. As these classes grow, they should be divided as illustrated in the following chart.

Notice that when two ages or grades are grouped together and use the same curriculum, it is necessary to cycle the material. For example, if you must group a third and fourth grade class together to study the same lesson one year, they should all study third-grade material. The next year they will study fourth-grade material. This system is called cycling the material.

The chart on Recommended Grouping for Children will help the administrator see the growth pattern of classes and departments and to see the relationship of Plan A and Plan B to the Children's division.

AS YOUR CHILDREN'S DIVISION GROWS
...divide your **CLASSES** as follows:

8 students 1 class	16 students 2 classes	24 students 3 classes	48 students 6 classes	96 students 12 classes
1 2 3 4 5 6	1 2 3 / 4 5 6	1 2 / 3 4 / 5 6	1 / 2 / 3 / 4 / 5 / 6	1 1 / 2 2 / 3 3 / 4 4 / 5 5 / 6 6

(Classes should not exceed 8 members, at which time a new class should be formed.)

...divide your classes to form **DEPARTMENTS** as follows:

For Sunday Schools with 2 grades in a department	For Sunday Schools with 4 or more classes in 2-grade groups	For Sunday Schools which have 2 or more classes per grade
Grades 1 2		
Grades 3 4	Grades 1 2	Grade 1 1 1
Grades 5 6	Grades 1 2	Grade 2 2 2
	Grades 3 4	Grade 3 3 .3
	Grades 3 4	Grade 4 4 4
	Grades 5 6	Grade 5 5 5
	Grades 5 6	Grade 6 6 6

GROUPING THE YOUTH DIVISION

Classes and department groupings in the Youth division have more often broken with traditional schedules than other age levels. You may group Youth classes in many ways, but in any case the ultimate criterion is whether or not we achieve our teaching/learning aims.

The following chart was designed to show how grouping might occur as classes are divided because of numerical growth. Notice the variety of ways Youth division classes can be grouped.

YOUTH DEPARTMENT/CLASS GROWTH					
A	B	C	D	OPTIONS	
7 8 9 10 11 12	7 8 9 / 10 11 12	7 8 / 9 10 / 11 12	7 / 8 9 10 / 11 / 12	7 8 / 9 10 11 12	7 8 / 9 / 10 11 12

Classes should not exceed 8-10 students.
Departments should not exceed 30-40 students.

When classes in this division meet together for an assembly, it will represent a Youth department. When classes in a department grouping teach different lessons, the assembly program will be unrelated to the Bible lesson aim, and therefore should be brief and pointed. All unnecessary material should be excluded. When there are two to three classes studying the same lesson we would recommend grouping them together into a department so that the total group can move to help achieve the teaching/learning aim. Two to three grades may be grouped in the Youth division and still use the same lesson material.

GROUPING THE ADULT DIVISION

Sunday School leaders have many diverse opinions on how to group adults. The basis for a grouping arrangement may be age, similarity of needs or the subject to be taught.

A basic need of adults is Christian fellowship, and Sunday School seems ideally suited to provide and encourage it. Experience seems to weigh heavily for grouping adults on the basis of age in order to achieve the fellowship goal. Since many needs are expressed by the age of the learner, it is possible to zero in on those needs in an age grouping.

Some churches have agreed that age grouping has many values, but they would also like to allow for more opportunities of instruction that is based on subject. Classes divided on the basis of subject are often referred to as elective classes.

The following chart indicates a grouping pattern by age and then two options are suggested to allow for choice of subject.

GROUPING CHART FOR ADULT DIVISION		
Three options:		
AGE	AGE WITH LIMITED ELECTIVES	ELECTIVES
College age-young adult 18-23	18-23 E	E E
Young adult 24-35	24-35 E	E
Middle adult 36-59	36-59	E E
Older adult 60-	60- E	E
Subdivide as necessary		Maintain age grouping for fellowship

PLAYBACK

1. Name the four basic age divisions in the Sunday School.

2. List the correct sizes for classes in each division.

3. Give definitions for a class, a department and a division.

4. Do the departments and classes in your own Sunday School meet the requirements for correct sizes? If not, what plans can you make to divide classes for more effective teaching/learning?

HOW TO USE THE HOUR

CAN YOU:

1. *List five reasons why the Sunday School teacher should have a clearly defined time schedule for each session?*
2. *Describe the session time schedule for each of the four major age divisions?*
3. *List the four divisions of time for an Adult Sunday School class?*

After reading chapter 6, you can.

Time is of essence in the Sunday School session. One hour a week is so little time to communicate so much. And many teachers have less than an hour of actual teaching time. The shortage of time allotted to Sunday School and the failure to achieve maximum use of that time often limits effective teaching. As you develop a teaching philosophy which requires time-consuming learner involvement activities, you must use wisely the small amount of time you have.

You, the administrator, can encourage maximum utilization of the time by implementing Total Session Teaching so that every portion of the hour is used in achieving the session aim. You can also urge your teachers to prepare a clearly defined schedule for each session. Your teachers will discover five major values in using such a schedule in their teaching:

1. They can maintain an adequate emphasis on both

Scripture and learner involvement. In their efforts to get learners actively involved in the session, they must not minimize the Bible content of the lesson.

2. They can plan systematic steps to reach the teaching/learning aim. The schedule will help them to remember that they are teaching for specific results.

3. They can maintain continuity throughout the class session. This continuity provides security for both teacher and learners.

4. They can see their priorities clearly. Teachers can then eliminate nonessential materials which might distract learners from moving toward the session aim.

5. They can choose the most appropriate learning activities for the session. When teachers have selected their session aims and have prepared a schedule for the hour, they can then more easily determine what teaching methods they should use. Methods should always be appropriate to the age group and to the aim you want to reach. (A complete list of teaching methods and how to use them is included in the *Ways to Help Them Learn* (Regal Books) series.

Because the needs of learners in the four major age divisions are different, the ways in which they spend the Sunday School hour should be different. The charts and descriptions in this chapter will help you distinguish between the different time schedules for each age division. You will need to study the schedules so that you can be familiar with the needs of all four age groups. The schedules are designed to insure maximum involvement for the learner as well as proper emphasis on the biblical content.

SCHEDULING THE EARLY CHILDHOOD DIVISION

The time schedule for your Early Childhood division should allow the teachers to communicate to each young child that he is special, even when part of a group. When he first arrives at the door of the classroom, he has an opportunity to express his individuality by choosing which activitiy he wants to participate in. While he works in small-group learning activities during this first segment of time, he receives lots of personal attention. He is then ready to join in the larger Together Time Group. And from there he moves to a small, permanent group where his teacher tells the Bible story. In this group the teacher encourages the child's participation and builds strong teacher-child relationships.

A good schedule is flexible, and teachers need to work at a relaxed, unhurried pace. They must be prepared to accommodate both early arrivers and latecomers into the Bible Learning Activities. With this schedule, Sunday School really does begin for each child whenever he arrives.

A good schedule must also be balanced. A variety of both quiet activities and more exciting activities will help teachers prevent boredom or overstimulation. The schedule also allows for a balance in group sizes. The child is involved in small groups for most activities, but for activities like group music he participates with a larger group. The schedule also achieves a balance between child activity and teacher instruction. Teachers weave aim-related conversation throughout the total program so that every experience the child has reinforces the desired learning.

The following schedule is designed to meet the needs of young children within a workable structure for either large or small departments.

EARLY CHILDHOOD DEPARTMENT SCHEDULES

BIBLE LEARNING ACTIVITY TIME	TOGETHER TIME	BIBLE STORY/ ACTIVITIES*
(Individual and small group activities. Children have free choice.)	(Full department together under leadership of department superintendent.)	(Small groups permanently assigned to specific teachers.)
2s Most of the hour	Maximum 5 minutes, if any	Included in Bible Learning Activities
3s 40-45 minutes	10-15 minutes	10-15 minutes
4s 30-35 minutes	15-20 minutes	15-20 minutes
5s 30-35 minutes	15-20 minutes	15-20 minutes
Each time sequence includes the time necessary for moving from one part of the schedule to the next.		*If Bible story is told in Together Time, subtract 5 minutes from Bible Story Activities and add to Together Time.

SCHEDULING THE CHILDREN'S DIVISION

A time schedule which will meet the needs of learners in grades 1 through 6 should provide:

1. Both small group and large group experiences.
2. Opportunities to make choices and to help plan Bible learning activities.
3. Opportunities to work with different children and teachers in the department.
4. Learning experiences which reinforce the lesson and unit aims.
5. Involvement in Bible learning activities which encourage Bible-related research and which help learners apply Bible truth in their daily lives.

Administrators should consider the two following time schedules which can be used in the Children's division. Both are designed to insure meaningful learning experiences for children. These schedules provide time to meet all the needs of children listed above.

Plan A — This plan divides the Sunday School hour into three blocks of time. (See chart, page 65.) Closely graded departments (one grade) and group graded departments (two grades using the same lesson materials) may use Plan A. This schedule includes time for large and small groups, choices and planning and involvement in meaningful Bible learning activities. The hour begins with Bible study as a basis for the total session and everything that follows reinforces and builds on that Bible truth. Notice carefully the differences in the first Sunday of a unit, the middle Sundays and the last Sunday.

Plan B — This plan divides the session into two blocks of time. (See chart, page 66.) Class groups, each studying a different grade level curriculum, may use Plan B and meet together at the end of the hour for Bible sharing time. The schedule includes time for Bible learning activities, involvement in large groups and small groups, choice making and planning. Every part of the hour contributes to reaching the lesson and unit aims.

Administrators should understand the developmental sequence of Bible learning activities. Notice that on the first Sunday the learners choose an activity and begin their planning and research for the activity. Research and

PLAN A

HOW TO USE YOUR TOTAL SESSION TEACHING TIME

BIBLE STUDY	BIBLE SHARING/ PLANNING	BIBLE LEARNING ACTIVITIES
This diagram represents the first block of time for the Sunday school period. It includes all the material to be used in the permanent class grouping. When the child arrives, he begins working on an activity that builds readiness for Bible learning. He then listens to the Bible story and thinks through ways of applying to his own life the truths he learned from God's Word.	This diagram represents the time when all the children in the department are together in a large group. Normally it will be the second time block in the Sunday school hour. All the children share together in worship and other large group activities. Then each child selects the Bible learning activity he wants to work on during the third block of time.	This diagram represents the block of time which normally is the last portion of the Sunday school period. Children are divided into small nonpermanent groups, according to the activities they choose to work on. A teacher leads each activity. Note that at this time the teacher does not work with his own class group, but rather with the children who choose the activity he is leading.

If you have 75 minutes

25-35 minutes	up to 15 minutes	20-25 minutes

If you have 60 minutes

25-30 minutes	up to 10 minutes	20 minutes

Note: *For review purposes of each unit, the last two blocks of time can be reversed —children go directly from class time to their Bible learning activities; then all could meet together for large group time. This would allow children to complete their Bible learning activities (small groups) and then to share what they learned during the unit (large group).*

PLAN B
ANOTHER WAY OF USING THE LESSON MATERIAL

BIBLE STUDY/BIBLE LEARNING ACTIVITIES 40 minutes (permanent class group)	BIBLE SHARING 15-20 minutes (department group)
Teacher uses suggestions in Bible Study time and chooses one Bible learning activity for his entire class to take part in.	Department Superintendent adapts material from Bible Sharing/Planning section. Music and conversation are thus an outgrowth and/or expression of what was learned in class time. Note that it will not be necessary to allow for planning and choosing Bible learning activities when material is arranged in this way.

work on the activity continues on the middle Sundays. On the last Sunday of the unit the learners complete their activity and share it with the group.

These time schedules in the Children's division require the teachers to work together as a team. To do so, they must spend regular time in planning together. Administrators need to guide and support their teachers in planning efforts.

CHECKPOINT: *Study both Plan A and Plan B and make a copy of the session time schedule for your Children's classes and/or departments. Is your own schedule like Plan A or B? Will Plan A or B meet the needs of your Children's division? What can you as an administrator do to insure that each part of the teaching/learning session involves the children in a meaningful learning experience?*

SCHEDULING THE YOUTH DIVISION
"How can we keep from getting into a rut?"

Youth leaders often ask questions like that. They don't

want class members to feel that every Sunday School session will be exactly the same in method or in schedule.

To provide variety and change of pace, the following charts offer six separate schedules. Teachers should choose the format which will best help them reach the lesson aim for a particular session.

Here's how teachers should decide which time schedule to use in each session:

1. Choose a passage of Scripture.

2. Determine the session aim for learners.

3. Select methods to lead learners to achieve the session aim.

4. Choose the time schedule which best supports the methods they have chosen.

The six arrangements for teaching are:

SIX ARRANGEMENTS FOR TOTAL SESSION TEACHING

1. Large group only

2. Small groups only

3. Large group, then small groups

4. Small groups, then large group

5. Small groups, large group, then small groups

6. Large group, small groups, then large group

This variety of Youth schedules allows time for both large group and small group participation. In Sunday Schools where more than one class is studying the same lesson, teachers will combine those classes for the large-group learning activities. Activities are offered which help learners reach the session aim. When only one class is studying a particular lesson, the teacher will divide the class into small groups for learning activities.

Remember that the maximum size for a Youth class is 8-10 learners for each teacher. A department maximum is 30-40 in attendance.

SCHEDULING THE ADULT DIVISION

The late Henrietta Mears, who taught hundreds of adult Bible classes during her lifetime, often stated that adults probably gather in study groups more for Christian relationships than any other single reason. People have a need for both fellowship and Bible study, and Adult Sunday School classes are an ideal place to bring the two together.

To emphasize fellowship, we should give specific time for it. The schedule for the Adult division classes should include a specific fellowship time either before, during or after the teaching/learning session. Here are the four divisions of time in Adult classes:

FELLOWSHIP	APPROACH	EXPLORATION	DECISION

A different part of the teaching/learning session is emphasized each week as the teacher determines the session aim. On the first Sunday of a unit, for example, a teacher may spend most of his time on the approach section, whereas on the last Sunday he would emphasize the decision section or life-related responses.

The three parts of the teaching/learning schedule for adults — approach, exploration and decision — will each in turn be emphasized during the unit. This changing emphasis provides flexibility and variety for both teacher and learner.

An Adult class should not exceed 25-40 learners in order for the teacher to provide an opportunity for exploration and discovery on the part of each learner in the class.

PLAYBACK

1. List five reasons why the Sunday School teacher should have a clearly defined time schedule for each session.

2. Describe the session time schedule for each of the four major age divisions.

3. List the four divisions of time for an Adult Sunday School class.

4. Do your Adult classes have a specific time for fellowship? How can you implement adult fellowship into your own Sunday School?

5. Do your Youth division classes use a variety of time schedules and formats? How can you, as administrator, encourage your Youth leaders to use different methods and schedules each week?

USING YOUR FACILITIES CREATIVELY

CAN YOU:
1. *Define an assembly/class design and an open-room design?*
2. *State the recommended number of square feet of floor space per learner in each of the four age-level divisions?*
3. *List the basic classroom requirements for all age levels?*

After reading chapter 7, you can.

The environment your teachers instruct in can be either an asset or a liability. It all depends on how they use their facilities. The teacher must create a stimulating learning environment — it won't just happen by itself. As an administrator it is your job to help your teachers understand the role of the environment in teaching/learning.

Everyday life situations are the best environment for teaching. All of Jesus' teaching was on-the-spot in the natural environment of His Jewish learners. His teaching situations included the Sea of Galilee, fishing boats, shepherds with their flocks, wells for drawing water, a marriage feast, the synagogue, sorrow over sickness, a funeral, a storm and a fig tree. Jesus used creatively the situations which the Jews confronted almost daily.

In the Old Testament Moses encouraged the Israelites to teach God's truth to their children in their own homes where they worked, played, rested and laughed. Learning was achieved in the environment of family relationships and experience.

The Sunday School teacher must begin in a sterile classroom, with four bare walls, and make it an exciting place to learn about God and His Word. It's a real challenge, but it's worth the effort in order to develop a learning environment which supports and enriches your teaching.

ASSEMBLY/CLASSROOM DESIGN

Many churches have constructed traditional facilities that have small classrooms leading off from a large assembly room. (See diagram.) This learning environment provides for small-class group instruction as well as large-group worship and other activities. This arrangement is especially suitable to a Sunday School which is organized on a class level.

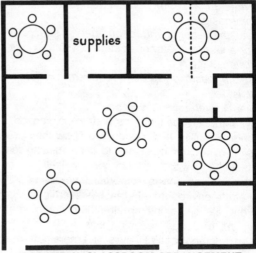

ASSEMBLY/CLASSROOM ARRANGEMENT

OPEN-ROOM DESIGN

Sunday Schools organized on a department or division level often prefer an open-room design for their classes. Instead of meeting in small adjoining classrooms, all the classes in a department meet in one large assembly room. The groups of learners work around tables placed in various parts of the room, and a teacher leads the activities at each table. This allows the teachers in a department to help each other, and to plan their lessons together as a team.

Learners have been conditioned to learning in an open room in public school, so they are not distracted by having other activities in the same room with them. In fact, experienced educators say open-room teaching cuts down on discipline problems with children. They tend to imitate the actions of one another and work more enthusiastically because everyone else is working. With open-room teaching the individual learner needs are met while, at the same time, group spirit is fostered in the department.

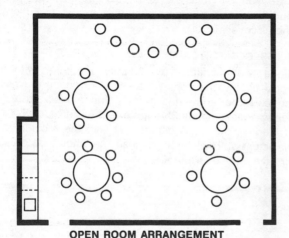

OPEN ROOM ARRANGEMENT

If your educational building is constructed on the assembly/class design and you would like to implement open-room teaching in some of your departments, you can adapt your facility. Remove the doors from the small classrooms or allow them to stand open during the teaching session. In addition to assigning Sunday School classes to the small classrooms, place two or more classes or activities in the adjoining assembly area at the same time. Encourage your department superintendents to direct, observe, evaluate and assist in learning activities. In this way they are active in the teaching/learning process.

Closed classroom doors too often lock superintendents out of their primary role of assisting and encouraging the teachers in their department.

One word of caution — classes that meet in open-room areas should be studying the same lesson so that a unified time schedule can be adapted.

ROOM SIZE AND FURNISHINGS

The size of the classroom and the way you furnish it depends on the age-group level and number of the learners in the class or department. As a rule, children need more room to move about during the session than do adults. A children's classroom should simulate his various everyday surroundings, while the adult classroom should provide study aids and resource materials for Bible exploration and discovery.

CLASSROOM FOR EARLY CHILDHOOD (AGES 1–5)

Since young children work, play and think with their whole bodies, their primary need is for space in which to move. Experience has shown that each young child needs approximately 35 square feet (an area of 5x7 feet) of learning space. A department with the recommended maximum of 24 children, for instance, should be no smaller than 840 square feet.

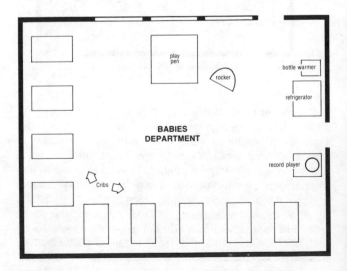

play pen

rocker

bottle warmer

refrigerator

BABIES DEPARTMENT

record player

Cribs

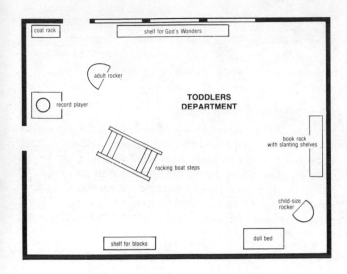

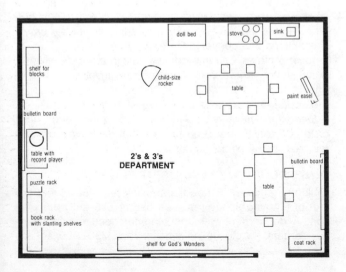

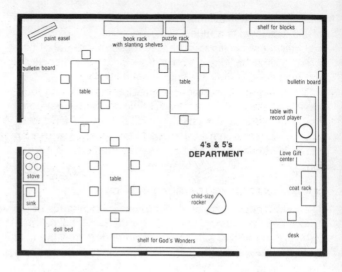

The room should be furnished in accord with valid teaching/learning techniques: block building, "God's wonders," books, puzzles, home living, story telling, music and art activities.

The ideal location for all early childhood departments is at ground level, with quick and easy access to the outside. Rooms on the first floor generally offer better safety precautions and convenience for parents.

Toilet facilities that immediately adjoin each room are a convenience where young children are involved. Fixtures should be child-sized. A sink and a drinking fountain in the department are also good investments.

Electrical outlets equipped with safety plugs and out of children's reach should be provided on each wall to avoid the hazards of extension cords.

CLASSROOM FOR CHILDREN (GRADES 1-6)

Children grades 1-6 need approximately 25–30 square feet of learning space (an area 5x5 or 5x6 feet) per person. A department with the recommended maximum of 30 learners should be no smaller than 750–900 square feet.

Equipping the classroom with learning aids appropriate to this age level is a must!

Under most circumstances it is recommended that children's rooms be located on a first- or second-floor level and near an exit opening onto a main corridor.

Other matters to consider are restrooms, drinking fountains and sinks. It is most desirable to place restrooms near all children's rooms. Having a sink or drinking fountain in the classroom is a great asset when you use art and construction activities as creative methods of instruction.

CLASSROOM FOR YOUTH (GRADES 7–12)

The youth classroom should provide a minimum of 15 square feet of learning space (an area 3x5 feet) per person. A department with the recommended maximum of 30–40 learners should be no smaller than 450–600 square feet. It must include resource materials for learners to discover biblical truths on their own and a place to practice what they are learning.

An entire class could meet in the church library on occasion. When it would help achieve the objective of a particular Sunday's session, this would be an unusual and welcome change. Learners should learn to locate and explore books, cassettes and other audiovisuals which are available there.

CLASSROOM FOR ADULTS (AGES 18 AND OVER)

The educational facilities for adults are important because the adult department of the Sunday School is strategic to the entire program of the local church. Ideally an adult classroom provides a minimum of 15 square feet of learning space (an area 3x5 feet) per person. A class with the recommended maximum of 30 learners should be no smaller than 450 square feet.

The adult classroom should also be equipped with study aids and resource materials suitable to the planned learning activities.

GENERAL REQUIREMENTS

Here are a few basic requirements for classrooms at all age levels. Classrooms should have the proper lighting, heating, cooling and ventilation. Good acoustics are also an asset. The walls of the classroom should be sound-proof, the ceiling acoustically treated, and the floor carpeted if possible. There should be electrical outlets located conveniently throughout the room for tape recorders, slide, filmstrip or motion picture projectors and overhead or opaque projectors.

Be sure each room contains sufficient chairs and tables of appropriate size for the age level of the class; cabinets or closets for storage; a permanent or a portable chalkboard for each classroom. There should be a tack board or a bulletin board for displaying visual aids. And if a class uses an overhead projector frequently, the room should be furnished with a permanet screen.

Additional details for equipping and using the classrooms as learning environments, can be found in the *Ways to Plan and Organize Your Sunday School* and *Ways to Help Them Learn* books for each age level (Regal Books).

ONE LAST PROBLEM

The biggest problem with developing creative environments for teaching is the often-heard cry: "But we can't afford that kind of building...or room...or equipment!" You may not be able to equip your facility perfectly overnight, but you must set your priorities and begin somewhere. Select some of the things which you can do right now and then plan what you can do over a short-range period and then over a long-range period. You can obtain the needed equipment gradually. You can remodel or adapt a building over a period of time. You can purchase items or receive them as gifts one at a time. As you set priorities, you are planning for growth. And you will see learning results as you begin to make these stimulating changes in your learning environment.

PLAYBACK

1. Define an assembly/class design. Define an open-room design.

2. State the recommended number of square feet of floor space per learner in each of the four age-level divisions.

3. List the basic classroom requirements for all age levels.

IT'S YOUR MOVE!

1. *Analyze your Sunday School classrooms for compliance with basic requirements of a good learning environment by completing the following chart.*

Room	Location	Adequate Space	Acoustics Good	Heating	Lighting	Tack Board	Chalkboard	Screen	Supply Area	Right Size Tables & Chairs

2. *Are your Youth and Adult classrooms adequately supplied with resources and study aids? If not, list the needed resources and plan how you can obtain them.*

3. *Are your Early Childhood and Children's classrooms adequately supplied with resources for learning activities appropriate to those age levels? If not, decide what is needed and how the need can be met.*

ORGANIZING THE SUNDAY SCHOOL

CAN YOU:
1. *Identify five Sunday School organizational patterns?*
2. *Name and describe the duties of each Sunday School leader?*
After reading chapter 8, you can.

Some people think that organization is unspiritual. It can be — if the only thing we care about is our organization, programs and techniques. Most of the people who don't like any organization at all are simply reacting to their past experiences where there was an overemphasis on organization. But it can be just as bad to have no organization at all. The apostle Paul instructed the Corinthian church, "Let all things be done properly and in an orderly manner" (1 Cor. 14:4), and "God is not a God of confusion but of peace, as in all the churches of the saints" (1 Cor. 14:33).

Every Sunday School needs just enough organization to prevent confusion — and no more. The amount of organization which you need will vary with each Sunday School. As administrator, it's your job to determine just how much organization your Sunday School needs.

The Bible calls the Church the body of Christ. Think of our physical bodies and the precision organization which causes all the organs, muscles, bones, tissues and blood vessels to work together. Yet without the spirit in the body there is no person or personality. God doesn't want chaos and confusion in His Church. But He also doesn't want the other extreme of a cold, lifeless superstructure.

Organizational standards should never be law — they are simply guidelines. As administrator, you should prayerfully set goals for your Sunday School. Then you must plan how to reach your goals. The purpose of organization is to help you accomplish your goals by limiting the span of control of each worker. Your goals should remain static, but you must be flexible enough to change your plans whenever necessary. It is also extremely important for you to communicate your goals and the rationale for your methods to all of your staff workers. They can function together as a team only if they know what their goals are and how best to arrive at them.

ORGANIZATIONAL PATTERNS

Sunday Schools are usually organized according to one of five basic patterns. Look closely at the description of each one below and identify which one matches the organizational pattern of your Sunday School.

1. Class
2. Class and Department
3. Department
4. Department and Division
5. Division

CLASS

In a Sunday School organized at the class level, there are no departments. Each class is led by a teacher who reports directly to the general superintendent. Smaller churches usually have class level Sunday Schools because they do not have enough classes in any one age group to make up a department.

CLASS LEVEL

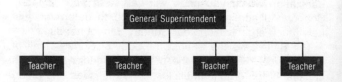

CLASS AND DEPARTMENT

In a class and department level Sunday School there are both Classes and Departments. There may be enough classes in some age levels to be able to create a department. Each department has a department leader who supervises the teachers in that department. The department leaders are responsible to the general superintendent. In the classes without departments the teachers report directly to the general superintendent. Class and department level Sunday Schools are also usually found in smaller and medium-sized churches.

CLASS/DEPARTMENT

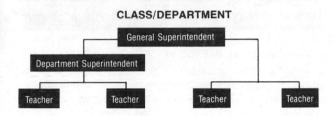

DEPARTMENT

A Sunday School may be completely departmentalized so that all classes in the church are grouped into departments. All teachers report to their department leaders, and the leaders in turn report to the general superintendent.

DEPARTMENT

General Superintendent

Department Superintendent — Department Superintendent — Department Superintendent

Teacher — Teacher — Teacher — Teacher — Teacher — Teacher

DEPARTMENT AND DIVISION

In a department and division level Sunday School, there are both departments and division. If there are four or more departments within one-age division, the Sunday School is organized on a divisional level. A division coordinator supervises the department leaders within his division and the coordinator reports to the general superintendent. In those age groups organized at the department level, the department leaders report to the general superintendent.

DEPARTMENT/DIVISION

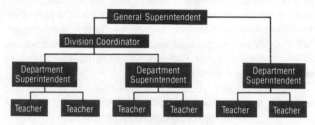

DIVISION

Some churches are large enough to be completely divisionalized. A divisionalized Sunday School indicates that each division has four or more departments. Each division has a division coordinator — one each for Early Childhood, Children, Youth and Adult. The division coordinators supervise the department leaders and report to the general superintendent. The division coordinator is a qualified layman, not a paid church staff member. His position is not the same as a Youth Director who supervises all activities of a certain age group and reports to the Director of Christian Education or the Christian Education Board.

DIVISION

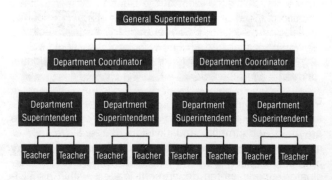

LEADERSHIP ROLES

The number of leaders you need depends on the number of people involved in your entire Sunday School. The best way to reach your goals is to limit the amount of work each leader is responsible for. An effective ratio is one leader for every five people being supervised. In this way one department leader supervises two to five teachers. One coordinator supervises two to five department leaders. A general superintendent supervises no more than five coordinators, department leaders or teachers.

As administrator, you need to select these leaders and teachers first on the basis of their spiritual gifts. Choose teachers who have demonstrated the spiritual gift of teaching. Choose leaders and coordinators who have the spiritual gift of administration.

One danger you must avoid is to advance a teacher to administrative responsibility just because he demonstrates effective teaching roles. A teacher may be skilled as a teacher and not be able to function in an administrative role. Administrators should seek people with organizational and administrative gifts for those positions which require these responsibilities.

The most familiar leadership positions in the Sunday School are: general superintendent, division coordinator, department leader, teacher and secretary. Administrators need to understand each of these roles in detail.

GENERAL SUPERINTENDENT

Most churches have a general officer who is responsible to the church for the work of the Sunday School. Usually, his title is General Superintendent. His is a very important position in the Sunday School ministry. As the elected or appointed leader of the Sunday School, he should be:

1. Guiding the other leaders in planning, conducting and evaluating their work.

2. Working with the leaders in enlisting personnel in accordance with church policy.

3. Communicating to the leaders the goals of the Sunday School.

4. Stimulating leaders in setting goals for achievement and in evaluating progress toward these goals.

5. Working with the leaders to insure an adequate

program of training for new teachers as well as in-service training for current staff.

6. Guiding leaders in determining and securing needed resources, both financial and physical, and evaluating the use of these resources.

7. Coordinating the Sunday School with other church agencies to develop a well-balanced program of Christian education.

8. Developing and maintaining divisions, departments and classes of the proper size and teacher-learner ratio.

9. Guiding teachers and leaders in a program of outreach to the unenlisted in the community.

10. Meeting monthly with division coordinators or department leaders for evaluation and planning.

SUNDAY SCHOOL DIVISION COORDINATOR

When a church has four or more departments within one-age level division, a division coordinator should be appointed. This officer is responsible to the general superintendent for all of the above functions within his division. The coordinator needs to be knowledgeable in Christian education, and he should work closely with the department leaders. He is personally involved in discovering, enlisting and training new staff members.

The division coordinator should have a deep concern for the Christian education of learners in the Sunday School and a keen awareness of how to make teaching/learning effective. This key position should be filled by a person of administrative ability, capable of guiding other people in their work. The coordinator's proper delegation of duties among his staff leaders is vital to his success.

The specific duties of the Sunday School division include:

1. Working within the framework of the church policy in discovering, recommending and enlisting personnel for the entire division.

2. Guiding department leaders in directing their teachers and secretaries in effective Sunday School ministry.

3. Functioning as the primary channel of communication between the Sunday School administration and the department leaders.

4. Representing the division at the monthly Sunday School council meeting.

5. Evaluating the space and equipment in the division and recommending needs to the general superintendent.

6. Developing and maintaining departments and classes of the proper size and teacher-pupil ratio by creating new departments and classes as growth occurs.

7. Guiding department leaders in a program of outreach in the community.

8. Meeting monthly with the department leaders for evaluation and planning.

9. Providing opportunities for training of prospective and present teachers and officers.

DEPARTMENT LEADER

The department leader can help teachers and secretaries most effectively by encouraging them and assuring them of his support in their ministry. He should be alert to the way the entire Sunday morning program is being conducted. He should express appreciation for jobs well done so that teachers will have a sense of satisfaction in their work. He should give constructive suggestions, tactfully, to his teachers. The department leader needs to encourage teachers to try new, well-planned techniques that will help them achieve a greater measure of success. He also needs to listen attentively to teachers' suggestions and complaints. He should attempt to implement constructive ideas.

In addition to this continual process of supervision and guidance, the leader should participate with teachers in training classes, conventions, workshops and individual study. Listed below are the department leader's general duties:

1. Discovering, recommending and enlisting personnel for the Sunday School department as he works within the framework of the church policy.

2. Helping department teachers and officers to fulfill their assignments.

3. Functioning as the channel of communication between the Sunday School general superintendent, or division coordinator, and teachers and secretaries.

4. Representing the department at the monthly Sunday School council meeting if there is no division coordinator.

5. Evaluating the space and equipment of the department and recommending needs to the coordinator or the general superintendent.

6. Building the proper ratio of teacher to learners by creating needed classes as growth occurs.

7. Leading in a program of outreach in order to find those in the community who are not enlisted in Sunday School.

8. Seeking to develop and maintain a plan in which the teachers effectively enlist the cooperation of the families of their learners in deepening the impact of the Sunday School's education ministry.

TEACHER

The teacher is of paramount importance because he personalizes God's Word to the lives of individual learners.

Every teacher needs a class small enough so that he can teach and cultivate each learner spiritually. Bible study and learning activities are more effective in the small-class group because teacher and learners can interact more. The small-class group also makes it easier for the teacher to sustain pupil attention and interest in the lesson and activities.

The following list of duties further defines the teacher's important role:

1. Guiding his class group in a life-related study of God's Word.

2. Guiding Bible learning activities for active and meaningful research and expression of study projects.

3. Cultivating the friendship and interests of learners and their families.

4. Leading learners into a progressive understanding of spiritual awareness and experience with Jesus Christ and His church.

5. Assisting the department leader in regular evaluation and planning at monthly department meetings.

6. Cooperating with the department leader and other teachers in an outreach ministry in the community.

7. Engaging in class and individual study opportunities that will improve his effectiveness.

8. Taking advantage of opportunities to improve his teaching.

ROLES AND RESPONSIBILITIES

OF SUNDAY SCHOOL LEADERS

GENERAL SUPERINTENDENT	DIVISION COORDINATOR	DEPARTMENT LEADER	TEACHER
1. Guides leaders in planning, conducting and evaluating their work.	1. Guides department leaders in planning, conducting and evaluating their work.	1. Guides teachers in planning, conducting and evaluating their work.	1. Guides leaders in Bible study with Bible learning activities, etc.
2. Recruits needed leaders for the Sunday School.	2. Recruits needed leaders for the division.	2. Recruits needed leaders for the department.	2. Refers possible leaders for the Sunday School to the department leader.
3. Secures resources for the Sunday School.	3. Defines resources needed for the division.	3. Defines resources needed for the department.	3. Defines resources needed for the class.
4. Helps leaders set goals for the Sunday School work.	4. Helps department leaders set goals for the work of the division.	4. Helps teachers set goals for the work of the department.	4. Helps learners set spiritual growth goals.
5. Provides training for the leaders of the Sunday School.	5. Provides training for the leaders in the division.	5. Provides training for the leaders in the department.	5. Takes advantage of the training provided for Sunday School leaders.
6. Coordinates the creation of new classes and departments as needed.	6. Creates classes and departments as needed in the division.	6. Creates new classes as needed in the department.	6. Builds class up to the maximum size so new classes can be formed.
7. Coordinates the outreach program for the Sunday School.	7. Coordinates the outreach program for the division.	7. Coordinates the outreach program for the department.	7. Cooperates in the outreach program for the department.
8. Conducts planning meetings for the Sunday School.	8. Conducts planning meetings for the division.	8. Conducts planning meetings (monthly) for the department.	8. Attends monthly planning meetings for the department.
9. Communicates to leaders policies, procedures and any changes in these.	9. Communicates to department leaders policies, procedures and changes in these.	9. Communicates to teachers policies, procedures and changes.	9. Keeps informed on changes in policies and procedures.
10. Coordinates with other church agencies for a total teaching ministry.	10. Coordinates all the division activities for a total program approach.	10. Coordinates department activities for a total teaching approach.	10. Cooperates with other leaders in the department for a total teaching approach.

SECRETARY

Numbers and records in the Sunday School are important because each one represents a person for whom Christ died. The secretary needs to keep track of information about these persons to make possible an orderly and effective ministry.

Generally he will be the first person that the learners see upon their arrival, and his friendly greeting may help to set the stage for a happy learning experience.

Very often he will have other opportunities through which he can personally minister in brief but meaningful ways to individual learners. His acquaintance with the records will enable him to know each class member by name and to encourage each one in Bible study and regular attendance of Sunday School sessions.

Here is a list of the secretary's duties:

1. Working in cooperation with the general Sunday School secretary and the department leader to maintain the records system.

2. Maintaining the department records system with accuracy.

3. Warmly greeting and welcoming learners from his desk near the entrance to the room.

4. Receiving, recording, reporting and submitting departmental offerings to the general Sunday School secretary.

5. Studying and analyzing the records, reporting any information that will help improve the department ministry.

6. Assisting in preparing absentee follow-up information and/or materials for the teachers.

7. Attending and participating in the monthly department planning meeting.

SPECIAL LEADERS IN THE ADULT DIVISION

The Adult Division has three special leaders — adult class leader, adult class unit leader and adult class social chairman.

The Adult Class Leader

Although the role of the adult class leader encompasses that of the traditional class president, it also goes beyond that.

1. The class leader is the primary administrator of the class. Under his direction the class does its part in achieving

the four objectives of the Sunday School.

2. He helps to keep the class "people-oriented" by working closely with the unit leaders in contacting and cultivating prospective class members.

3. He shares planning responsibilities with the teacher for coordinating the entire class session.

4. He is the primary channel of communication between the Sunday School's administrative staff and the individual class.

5. As class administrator, he interprets the job descriptions for the other class leaders and helps them fulfill their duties.

The Adult Class Unit Leader

The adult class unit leader is an important position.

1. A unit leader functions as sort of an undershepherd. The members of his unit are his flock. This concept should be clarified. The unit leader is not in competition with the pastor. The terms "undershepherd" and "flock" when applied to the unit leader refer to attitude, not office. He gets to know his unit members personally and is sensitive to their physical and spiritual needs.

The pastor should feel a sense of relief in knowing that there are other people who have genuine concern for members in the adult Sunday School classes. And as the unit leader ministers to his unit members, he should be sensitive to problems needing pastoral care. When he becomes aware of such problems, he should quickly alert the pastor concerning these needs.

2. The unit leader functions as a channel of communication, motivation and activation between the class leader and the unit members. The class leader looks to him to involve his unit members in class service projects and social activities.

3. When a new person begins attending the Sunday School class, he is placed into a unit by the class secretary.

The unit leader welcomes the new member and helps him feel comfortable in the group. He makes sure the newcomer is introduced to the other unit members, as well as to the other class members. At class social functions the unit leader makes sure that any newcomers to his unit are integrated into the larger group.

4. On Sunday mornings and at out-of-class activities the unit leader makes a mental note of who in his unit is absent. He then contacts these absentees and expresses his love and concern for them. He is vital in making people feel wanted and accepted in the group.

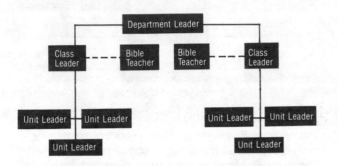

The Adult Class Social Chairman

The adult class social chairman also has an important role to fulfill:

1. The social chairman, who is directly responsible to the class leader, provides the leadership in planning social activities for the entire class. These social activities should take place on a regular basis — perhaps monthly.

The chairman provides the leadership in planning, but he doesn't do all the work! He should delegate much of the responsibility to other class members. In this way each class member has a ministry to the rest of the class, and each class member plays an important role in helping to achieve the four objectives of the adult Sunday School.

2. One of the reasons for limiting the size of an adult class is to assure maximum involvement of the members for both in-class and out-of-class activities. The social chairman should give each person an opportunity to be actively involved in the social functions. The class social times should

be structured so that members and visitors have the opportunity to get to know one another. Class socials should be a time of deepening interpersonal relationships.

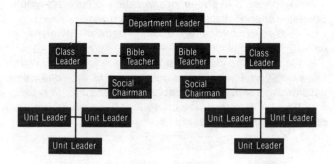

PLAYBACK

1. Beside each of the organizational patterns listed below, draw the appropriate organization chart and label each position you show on the chart.

DEPARTMENT AND DIVISION

DIVISION

CLASS

DEPARTMENT

CLASS AND DEPARTMENT

2. Name each of the Sunday School leaders and briefly describe his duties.

IT'S YOUR MOVE

1. Which of the above organization charts fits your Sunday School? Would another pattern work as well for you? Have you ever tried another pattern? What happened?

2. Compare the duties assigned to the leaders in your Sunday School with the duties listed in this chapter. Which things should your leaders be doing that they are not? Which things are they doing that they should not be doing, but should delegate to someone else?

PLANNING MEETINGS

CAN YOU:
1. *List four basic types of meetings and state who attends each?*
2. *State the kinds of planning meetings needed in a class level Sunday School? A department level? A division level?*
3. *Describe the function of the Christian Education Committee?*
After reading chapter 9, you can.

In order for our bodies to function smoothly, the various members of the body must work together. This interdependency is just as necessary in the body of Christ as it is in our physical bodies. In the Sunday School the members of Christ's body work together better if they also plan together.

Planning is not as complicated or as boring as it sometimes sounds. In fact, we do it every day without even thinking about it. When a man's car breaks down, he plans how to fix it. When a woman's pot roast burns, she plans hurriedly what else to serve. Buying groceries or buying a car also involve planning. Planning is a bridge between what is and what could be. For teachers and learners, building the bridge takes time and effort, but the results are worth it.

PURPOSE OF PLANNING MEETINGS

It is the responsibility of the administrator to make certain that the time in planning meetings is used wisely. In traditional planning meetings most of the time is given to business or inspiration. These elements are valuable, but the most important reason for requiring your teachers to meet regularly is to give them an opportunity to plan their lessons together. Actual preparation of lessons is the main purpose for holding Sunday School planning meetings.

Since your lessons are divided into units of study, it is essential that your teachers meet together to plan at least once per unit. They need to talk about their goals for each lesson and for the unit and about the best methods for reaching those goals.

It is especially important in department and divisional level Sunday Schools that teachers plan together when there is more than one teacher teaching the same lesson. Even in a class level Sunday School teachers should have plenty of time in planning meetings to actually prepare their lessons.

WHY PLAN TOGETHER?

Your teachers and leaders will plan more effectively if they plan together. Their planning can be exciting as they share needs and problems and pray for each other. These meetings should be a time of in-depth fellowship and communication among your staff members. But for effective planning, the staff must go beyond problems, fellowship and announcements. They must actually work together to prepare their lessons. As they plan their lessons as a team, they will stimulate each other's thinking and encourage creativity in teaching. Newer teachers can benefit from the knowledge and ability of more experienced teachers.

In these planning meetings your teachers' spiritual gifts will complement each other. Most teachers have other spiritual gifts in addition to teaching. As they plan their Bible lessons together, one teacher with the gift of exhortation may encourage a disheartened teacher who is having problems with his class. Another teacher may minister the gift of wisdom, another knowledge, another discernment, another faith, and so on. In this way the Holy Spirit is ministering to all your leaders and teachers as they exercise their gifts with each other. That's how Christ wants His body to function. These planning meetings can be the sturdy bridge to an exciting people-oriented Sunday School ministry led by the Holy Spirit.

TYPES OF MEETINGS

There are four types of planning meetings you may need to use: Sunday School council, general staff, divisional and departmental. The charts on pages 101-103 will help you to determine which of these meetings you need to have in your own Sunday School.

CHECKPOINT: *Identify the level on which your Sunday School is organized (see chapter 8). Your Sunday School organization level will determine which types of meetings you should hold.*

If your Sunday School is organized at the class level, see chart #1, page 101.

If your Sunday School is organized at the department level, see Chart #2, page 102.

If your Sunday School is organized at the division level, see Chart #3, page 103.

If your Sunday School is organized at a combination of any two of the above, see both of the appropriate charts.

OTHER MEETINGS
ADULT CLASS OFFICERS

Because they need to be aware of plans for the Sunday School, the adult class officers should attend the general staff or divisional planning meetings. When the rest of the Sunday School leaders break up for department meetings, these officers hold their own separate meeting.

If the Adult Division is on the elective system or if each adult class is studying a different lesson, then the Bible teacher can also meet with the class officers during their meeting.

The following items would be included in their agenda: How do we reach adults? How do we care for adults? How do we minister to adults? How do we help the caring units plan to minister? What do we need to do about class operations?

CHRISTIAN EDUCATION COMMITTEE

Some churches have a Christian Education Committee or Board, instead of a Sunday School council. This committee sets policies for all the church programs, including the Sunday School.

If the Christian Education Committee is composed of representatives from all of the church programs, it can become an effective coordinating and planning agency. It can clarify objectives, coordinate the overall church calendar and eliminate overlap or duplication of effort.

Because the Sunday School includes about 80 percent of the leaders in the church program, Sunday School representation on the committee should be weighted accordingly. Unfortunately, the Sunday School in some churches has no representation at all on the committee. This is a problem because those who determine Sunday School policies should be those who are involved in the weekly teaching process.

The meeting should probably be chaired by the Director of Christian Education, assisted by the Sunday School general superintendent, in order to function effectively in place of the council.

PLAYBACK

1. List four basic types of meetings and state who attends each.

2. State the planning meetings needed in a class level Sunday School. A department level. A division level.

3. Describe the function of the Christian Education Committee.

IT'S YOUR MOVE

1. How many Sunday School planning meetings have you attended in the last three months? Look at your church calendar for this month. How many planning meetings are scheduled? Which ones will you attend?

2. How can you best prepare for the next Sunday School planning meeting you will attend?

3. How should you plan for the next Sunday School planning meeting you will conduct?

LINCOLN CHRISTIAN COLLEGE AND SEMINARY

PLANNING MEETINGS FOR THE
CLASS
LEVEL SUNDAY SCHOOL

TYPE OF MEETING	FREQUENCY	WHO ATTENDS	AGENDA ITEMS
Sunday School Council	Quarterly (or monthly)	Conducted by the general superintendent. General superintendent and 3-5 teachers selected to represent the entire teaching staff. (Selection may be by appointment or election. Term may be from 6 months to 2 years.)	Discussion of overall calendar. Discussion of special problem areas such as personnel shortages, facility changes, record keeping. Policy setting for the Sunday School.
General Staff	Monthly immediately following the Sunday School Council meeting	Conducted by the general superintendent. General superintendent and all Sunday School leaders and workers.	General announcements regarding the Sunday School calendar. Promotion of special events: e.g., graduation dates, promotion day, curriculum ordering and receiving dates, special thrusts, missionary availabilities, appreciation banquets, all-church picnics, training seminars. Report of the Sunday School Council meeting by the general superintendent.
Divisional	Monthly immediately following the general staff meeting	Conducted by a designated person at each age level. All Sunday School staff working within each age level division meet together: e.g., there will be 4 separate meetings occurring simultaneously.	Brief inspirational talk. General motivation for more effective teaching, visitation. Specific application and interpretation of information for each age level. Discussion of the details of the teaching ministry for the specific age level. Teaching improvement, ways to plan a lesson or unit. Training and practice in the use of learning activities appropriate to the specific age level. Discussion of the overall education philosophy and policies adopted by the Sunday School Council.

PLANNING MEETINGS FOR THE
DEPARTMENT
LEVEL SUNDAY SCHOOL

TYPE OF MEETING	FREQUENCY	WHO ATTENDS	AGENDA ITEMS
Sunday School Council	Quarterly (or monthly)	Conducted by the general superintendent. General superintendent and all department leaders.	Discussion of overall calendar. Discussion of special problem areas such as personnel shortages, facility changes, record keeping. Policy setting for the Sunday School.
General Staff*	Monthly immediately following the Sunday School Council meeting.	Conducted by the general superintendent. General superintendent and all Sunday School leaders and workers.	General announcements regarding the Sunday School calendar. Promotion of special events: e.g., graduation dates, promotion day, curriculum ordering and receiving dates, special thrusts, missionary availabilities, appreciation banquets, all-church picnics and training seminars. Report of the Sunday School Council meeting by the general superintendent.
Departmental**	Monthly (weekly for best results). If monthly, immediately following the general staff meeting.	Conducted by department leaders. Each department leader meets with the secretary and teachers within his department.	Planning the unit. Planning the sessions: choosing learning activities to use, assigning specific responsibilities for the session. Discussion of and prayer about problems specific to the department. Practice with new learning activities. Training in educational philosophy specific to the age level.

*You may substitute a divisional meeting for the general staff meeting if desired. (See chart #1.)
**A department is defined as two or more classes studying the same lesson, grouped together into a department under a department leader.

PLANNING MEETINGS FOR THE
DIVISION
LEVEL SUNDAY SCHOOL

TYPE OF MEETING	FREQUENCY	WHO ATTENDS	AGENDA ITEMS
Sunday School Council	Quarterly (or monthly)	Conducted by the general superintendent. General superintendent and division coordinators.	Discussion of overall calendar. Discussion of special problem areas, such as personnel shortages, facility changes, record keeping. Policy setting for the Sunday School.
Divisional	Monthly immediately following the Sunday School Council meeting.	Conducted by division coordinators. All Sunday School staff working within each age level division meet together: e.g., there will be four separate meetings occurring simultaneously. Or, division coordinators meet with their department leaders, who then relay the information to teachers during the department meeting.	Brief inspirational talk. General motivation for more effective teaching, visitation. Specific application and interpretation of information for each age level. Discussion of the details of the teaching ministry for the specific age level. Teaching improvement, ways to plan a lesson or unit. Training and practice in the use of learning activities appropriate to the specific age level. Discussion of the overall education philosophy and policies adopted by the Sunday School Council. General announcements and promotions.
Department-mental*	Monthly (weekly for best results). If monthly, immediately following the divisional meeting.	Conducted by department coordinators. Each department leader meets with the secretary and teachers within his department.	Planning the unit. Planning the sessions: choosing learning activities to use, assigning specific responsibilities for the session. Discussion of and prayer about problems specific to the department. Practice with new learning activities. Training in educational philosophy specific to the age level.

*A department is defined as two or more classes all studying the same lesson, grouped together into a department under a department leader.

HOW TO RECRUIT AND TRAIN LEADERS

CAN YOU:
1. *State the training needs of Sunday School leaders? List five ways to provide training?*
2. *Explain the ways to train leaders for a major change in Sunday School?*
3. *Explain how to upgrade the teaching skills of your staff?*
After reading chapter 10, you can.

God has gifted various members of Christ's body for leadership. Your Sunday School has specific leadership needs, and God has placed in your church believers whom He has gifted for leadership. Your job as Sunday School administrator is to locate those people and train them, enabling them to exercise their gifts. As an administrator gifted to work with people, you must, under the leadership of the Holy Spirit, seek to guide gifted people into positions of leadership where they can minister most effectively.

HOW TO FIND LEADERS

You are like the controller in the tower at an airport. He knows what planes need to land and what landing space is available for them. He is the only person at the entire airport who can bring the two together. In the same way you as Sunday School administrator must have a clear picture of your entire church situation. You must be thoroughly familiar with every leadership position in your Sunday School and also with the people in your church who can fill those positions.

1. *Know the adults in your church.*

Get to know them personally as much as possible. If your church is extremely large, you may have to rely on the help of other source people to learn the gifts and abilities of all the members of your church. The pastor usually knows many of the members through visiting in their homes, meeting with new members and counseling. Because the adult Sunday School is the largest source of potential leadership, you can locate qualified leaders there by talking to your own teachers and officers in that department. Encourage your adult staff to be on the lookout for potential leaders and to refer names of those people to you constantly. Sometimes you may want to describe leadership needs to your church congregation and invite interested people to talk to you. If you make these announcements on a regular basis, instead of just when the vacancies arise, you can get to know people and train them in advance of the time you actually need them. That way you are prepared when an unexpected vacancy occurs. You also have more time to be sure you fill each vacancy with the right person.

2. *Know the specific requirements of every position of leadership in your Sunday School.*

Frequently leadership roles and responsibilities are misunderstood by both the recruiter and those who are being recruited. A carefully designed job description needs to be developed to assist in clarifying exactly what is expected of each prospective worker. Note the job requirements listed in chapter 8 of this book. As you decide on the particular requirements of each leader, be sure you know what the Bible says about the qualifications for leadership in any church. You should also be familiar with your own church's policies and procedures for selection and appointment of leaders.

3. *Pray.*

To do your job of leading people to positions where they can minister to the body of Christ, you must pray much. It is Christ's body, and He knows better than anyone else how it will function best. He wants to communicate that knowledge to you, but you must be willing to lift the needs up to Him and then listen to His direction. When you really rely upon Him, you will see marvelous results in your ministry.

4. *Approach people with a positive attitude.*
Recruiting leaders can be exciting. Don't beg people to take on jobs because you need to fill empty spaces or because it's their duty. Don't club them with a sense of responsibility. Instead, motivate them to get excited about being part of such a miraculous ministry. Inspire them by sharing how spiritual gifts work. Some shy people don't know they have a spiritual gift and can't believe God could really use them in any kind of ministry. Others are eager to serve, but they lack training or experience. Encourage the timid ones and offer training to the inexperienced.

HOW TO TRAIN LEADERS
Training is never a one-time effort, or even a yearly effort. Just as you must be continually recruiting leaders even before the need arises, you must provide continual training for all your leaders. Everything changes constantly — teaching staff, learners, culture, society, methods, organization and needs. In order for your Sunday School to be prepared to meet all these changes, your training must be a continuing program.

Your workers need several different kinds of training. New teachers and leaders need orientation to your organization, educational philosophy and training methods. Your current staff members need to constantly upgrade their teaching skills and their knowledge. All Sunday School leaders and teachers need training in basic educational philosophy, organizational principles, objectives of the Sunday School and the basics of how to personalize learning. For this training you can teach the entire staff together. But they also need specific training relating to the age group with which they work. For instance, the specialized needs and learning methods common for Adults are very different from those of Early Childhood, Children and Youth. For this training in age-level characteristics, you must separate them into the four age-level divisions.

Here are five excellent ways to provide your Sunday School staff with all the different kinds of training they need:

1. Observing and assisting.
2. Departmental planning meetings.
3. Divisional clinics.
4. Individualized instruction.
5. In-depth seminars.

OBSERVING AND ASSISTING

Every new leader needs some orientation in your Sunday School before taking on the responsibility for a class or department, even if he has had experience in teaching elsewhere. The best way to orient a new teacher or leader is to let him observe and assist for several weeks in the department he will be working in. He can simply observe, or he can help with secretarial duties. He should be included in all planning meetings for that department. After observing for a few weeks, he should join with the learners as a participant in the Bible learning activities. When he is comfortable with the procedures in your Sunday School, he will be ready for the responsibility of a class or department. In this way you are using your experienced teachers and leaders as your trainers.

Choose the most capable teacher or department in each division of your Sunday School for this training activity. Ask the teacher or department leader to assist you in the training ministry by accepting new teachers for observation and assisting assignments.

DEPARTMENTAL PLANNING MEETINGS

The departmental planning meetings are probably the best continuing training opportunity available to you. Since your leaders are already assembled on a regular basis, plan for training at every meeting! At this time you can initiate and train staff to cope with changes which affect the entire staff. During these planning meetings you can change attitudes and continually upgrade the skills of your leaders.

You may also clarify organizational principles and educational philosophy to help teachers understand grouping, time procedures, lesson preparation, adapting curriculum and teaching/learning process.

An easy and excellent way to provide this type of training is to present a summary of the information from one chapter of a selected resource book (e.g., *Ways to Plan and Organize Your Sunday School,* Regal Books) at each planning meeting. Afterwards, you could lead a discussion on the ideas presented.

Introduce, demonstrate and practice new Bible learning activities so teachers develop new skills. Discuss and evaluate previously used activities. Discuss age-group characteristics so teachers can better understand and reach their learners.

Each of the leaders has an opportunity to express ideas and opinions in these department meetings. They can discuss problems freely because all of them are working with the same type of learners. They can also be specific in how to deal with the problems and challenges. As you lead teachers in discussing and solving problems, you can train them in problem-solving techniques.

The key purpose of every department planning meeting is to prepare for the upcoming unit of study. As teachers systematically plan each unit and each Sunday's session, they learn to work together as a team. They also learn to plan good sessions effectively, to share responsibility and to personalize the lesson to meet the needs of the learners.

If department leaders have been properly trained, they will conduct the meeting so that each teacher learns the principles and skills which go into the making of an effective teacher. As teachers practice in these meetings, they discover and become comfortable with new teaching and planning techniques.

DIVISIONAL LEVEL CLINICS

You can help implement change in your Sunday School by providing divisional level clinics. You may schedule these clinics for several consecutive nights, for several consecutive Sunday evenings or for a weekend retreat or conference. Choose the plan which best meets the needs of your leaders.

In divisional level clinics you can provide continuing

education to your current leaders and assist them in upgrading their teaching skills.

You could use the ICL Regal kits as resource materials and textbooks for these sessions. There is one kit for each age level on *Ways to Plan and Organize Your Sunday School,* and another for each age level on *Ways to Help Them Learn.* Studies on Bible learning activities are available for the Children and Youth divisions as well.

To prepare for a divisional clinic, distribute the selected textbooks and learning guides to those who will participate. Then assign them to read chapters in the text and to complete the corresponding questions in the learning guide. The participants will then come to each session of the clinic prepared to discuss the concepts to be studied and to ask questions regarding unclear ideas.

INDIVIDUALIZED INSTRUCTION

In addition to observing and assisting, your new leaders will need some instructional training. They will, of course, attend your divisional level clinics and in-depth seminars as they are scheduled, but meanwhile you can use individualized instruction. You or another trained teacher may instruct them according to the training plan you have developed.

The ICL learning kits on the various age levels are one resource for this training. These kits provide a text, a learning guide and a cassette with study instructions. Give a new teacher one of these or other similar kits of your own choosing and assign him one or two chapters a week. Then meet with him once a week to review his answers in the learning guide and discuss the concepts he has studied.

IN-DEPTH SEMINARS

Another resource for training when you plan major changes in your Sunday School is the conference conducted for the benefit of several churches in an area. Some cities hold yearly conferences of this type under the auspices of the National Sunday School Association.

Another approach of this nature is the International Center for Learning, which sponsors regional seminars on Sunday School leadership education. Founded in 1970, this educational institution features proven successful concepts and methods, instruction by skilled leaders, helpful resource material, use of the latest media, personal counseling, comprehensive and in-depth study, guidance for successful evangelistic ministries and spiritual motivation. The spectrum of churches and Sunday Schools — from the large, well-equipped city church to the small, one-room rural mission with limited facilities — is included in the scope of the Center's program. Valuable training is provided to meet the needs of each of these situations.

You may also use the in-depth seminars to upgrade the skills and increase the knowledge of your teachers. Instructors in these seminars are outstanding Christian educators who specialize in particular age-level divisions.

Cost of the seminars may be paid by the individual leaders, by the church where possible or shared by the two.

ADDITIONAL TRAINING RESOURCES

You may supplement the above training methods with these general aids:

1. Outside reading in selected Christian education books.

2. Subscriptions to Christian education publications.

3. Correspondence courses on teaching or other Christian education subjects.

4. Christian education evening courses from a local Bible college.

5. Attendance at local or regional Sunday School conventions.

PLAYBACK

1. Describe the training needs of Sunday School leaders and list five ways to provide that training.

2. How do you train leaders for a major change in your Sunday School?

3. How do you upgrade the teaching skills of your staff?

IT'S YOUR MOVE!

1. What type of training did you receive for your present position in the church? Was it sufficient? What other training did you need before you started the job? What training do you still need?

2. How can you obtain that needed training? List the steps you will take to acquire the training you need. When will you do it?

3. Meet individually with the Sunday School leaders who report to you. Ask them about their training needs. In what area do they want help? Plan how and when you can help them receive the training they need. Follow up on the plan.

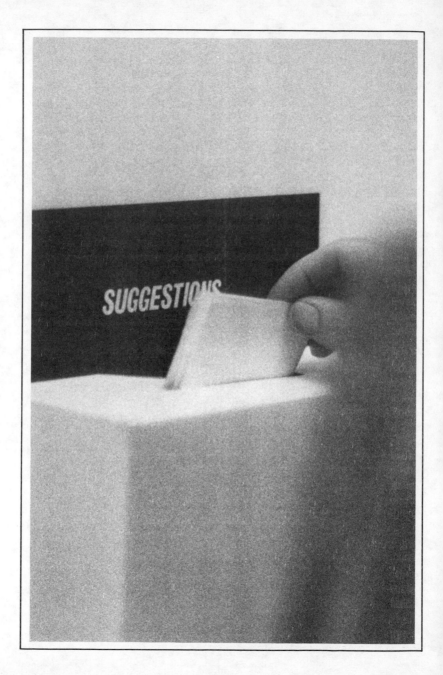

EVALUATING YOUR SUNDAY SCHOOL

CAN YOU:
1. *Write four reasons why you should evaluate your Sunday School?*
2. *Describe the elements of the Sunday School which can be evaluated?*
3. *Give three evaluation techniques?*
After reading chapter 11, you can.

Just because you have set goals and are progressing toward them doesn't mean you will automatically reach them. Sometimes an administrator gets off to a great start and his Sunday School makes progress for a while. He implements effective teaching/learning methods. He sets goals and encourages team planning. He provides the right amount of organization. He recruits and trains capable leaders. Even though he has gotten off to a good beginning, one major problem suddenly arises. Then before he can resolve that problem, another turns up in a different area. And then something else goes wrong, and soon all the progress comes to a halt, buried in the unsolved problems.

This administrator made only one basic mistake. When he began to see progress, he relaxed. He failed to evaluate his Sunday School program along the way so that he could anticipate problem areas and resolve them before they grew to overwhelming proportions.

WHY EVALUATE?

You need to evaluate your Sunday School program for the following specific reasons:

1. To check its effectiveness. Is your Sunday School reaching the objectives you have set for it?

2. To check its efficiency. Is the Sunday School meeting its objectives in the best and least complicated manner, while still maintaining a high level of effectiveness?

3. To learn where the needs are. If you are successfully solving problems in your Sunday School, the areas which need immediate attention will constantly be changing. So evaluation of the areas of need is a continual process. Where should you concentrate your efforts for the next few weeks? What problems are most important now? You will need a system for setting priorities so that you will be able to deal with new problems as they arise.

4. To decide where to set new goals. As you identify areas of need and plan how to meet those needs, you are actually setting short-term goals. As these goals are met, you will constantly be setting new ones.

WHAT TO EVALUATE

Evaluation should be extended to every part of the Sunday School program and every level of responsibility. In fact, the success of the evaluation will be determined by how specific the evaluation is. If you ask yourself, "Are we teaching the learners?" you will probably get an affirmative answer. But what part of the teaching is effective and what parts could be improved? How else will you know, unless you evaluate the specifics of the teaching program? Therefore, you and your Sunday School staff should evaluate the following kinds of details:

1. The facilities: equipment, room design, which classes are assigned to which classrooms, lighting, temperature, need for painting or repairs.

2. The communications: laterally — between the various staff members; upwards — from learners to teachers, teachers to superintendents and others; and downwards — from the general superintendent to the superintendents and on down to the teachers and others.

3. The staffing ratios: Are the classes the best size? Are the superintendents supervising from one to five teachers? Are the divisional coordinators over one to five superintendents?

4. *The leaders:* Are the leaders satisfied with their "assignments"? Do some want to rotate and work with another age level? Are there problems which need to be discussed? What about the working relationships?

5. *The sessions:* Are there problems? Should the session be lengthened, the order of the blocks of time be switched, the responsibilities changed?

6. *The curriculum:* Is the current curriculum still meeting the need? Are the illustrations appropriate? Is the content at the proper level for the learners?

7. *The planning meetings:* Are they frequent enough, conducted correctly, covering the right material, a waste of time? Are enough leaders in attendance? Should the meeting date be changed?

8. *The training:* Is more needed than is being provided? Is a different type of training needed? Who should conduct the training? Which type of training seems to be the most effective?

9. *The attendance:* Which classes show a high rate of absenteeism? Why? What percent of the enrollment of the entire Sunday School is in regular attendance? How can the percentage be increased? How can the enrollment be increased?

10. *The interest:* Do the learners seem interested in the classes? Which methods do they like best? Which methods do they seem to learn the most from? How is the interest shown? Should an open-room arrangement be introduced to solve discipline problems?

11. *The Sunday School objectives:* What things should the Sunday School accomplish? How? When? In what way and to what degree? Do you want to continue with the same basic objectives or do you feel you should change the emphasis of the Sunday School in your own church?

These items are only suggestions. Only you can decide what to evaluate in your own Sunday School. You must also select the best method and time for evaluation.

HOW TO EVALUATE

You must decide which evaluative device will be most useful in determining the effectiveness and efficiency of your own Sunday School. Here are three effective methods.

1. Check the statistics.
2. Solicit feedback from the staff and the learners.
3. Set specific measurable short-term goals.

CHECK THE STATISTICS

Your Sunday School records are filled with valuable statistics which will help you evaluate.

What is the total enrollment? What percentage of that enrollment is in regular attendance? Which classes show the highest percentage in attendance? Which show the lowest rate in attendance? What is the census of the neighborhood around the church? What percent of the available population in the area attend your Sunday School?

What has been the rate of growth of your Sunday School over the last year? Which classes have grown the fastest? Which have not grown? What effect has starting new classes had on the growth rate?

How much and what type of personal contact have the Sunday School leaders made over the last three months? How many personal visits? How many telephone calls? How many postcards were sent out? Did the attendance increase in those classes with the most personal contacts?

Analyze these statistics and present your conclusions and recommendations to the Sunday School staff.

SOLICIT FEEDBACK FROM THE STAFF AND THE LEARNERS

You will get a good idea of the attitude and feelings of the people in your Sunday School if you encourage feedback from them. You need not be tied down by the complaints and suggestions made by the learners and the staff. But listen attentively to the opinions expressed and be guided by them whenever possible.

You can get feedback from a suggestion box (no complaints please, without a suggestion for a solution!!!); a questionnaire checklist; or an opinionnaire with "stub end questions" for the staff and/or the entire Sunday School to complete.

Informal feedback should be encouraged in staff meetings, planning meetings and at any time during the week.

SET SPECIFIC, MEASURABLE, SHORT-TERM GOALS

Once a need is determined, the group of leaders involved should work as a group and set up a plan of action. Each step would be specific, measurable and have a due date. A time to evaluate the plan and the action should be set and followed through. You might use a project board for those projects which will take a period of one quarter or more. This will be a visual reminder of the project and a reassurance of the progress being made. At any one time, you will know exactly where you are going, where you are now and what is left to do.

Once this process is organized and operational, it is the easiest and most efficient way to accomplish the objectives of the Sunday School.

WHEN TO EVALUATE

If a problem arises, you will of course evaluate the cause and possible solutions right then. But the major items in the Sunday School program also need periodic evaluation.

For example, you might evaluate the space assignments, curriculum and leaders once a year — probably a few months before promotion and the new "year" starts. For most churches, the new year starts in September, concurrent with the beginning of the secular school year. So plan the evaluation for the summer so that you allow enough time to initiate changes as a result of the evaluation.

Short-term goals should be set on a quarterly basis for most projects. Therefore, you should evaluate them every quarter and set new goals or extend the time on the current ones.

Evaluating is like mowing the lawn. If you keep it up, it isn't too much of a problem, but if you let it go, the task becomes monumental!

PLAYBACK

1. Write four reasons why you should evaluate your Sunday School.

2. Describe the elements of the Sunday School which can be evaluated.

3. Give three evaluative techniques you might use in your Sunday School.

IT'S YOUR MOVE

1. *What about your Sunday School? When was the last time your staff evaluated their program? What did they evaluate? How? What areas did they forget to evaluate?*

2. *When did you last evaluate your area of responsibility in the Sunday School? What methods did you use? What plans for change did you make after that evaluation? Did your plans result in needed changes?*

3. *Evaluate an area of your responsibility for efficiency and effectiveness. Set three quarterly goals to improve your efforts in that area. List the specific steps you will take to reach your goals within a set period of time. Plan when and how you will evaluate your progress. Begin working on your plan. Stick to it! Follow through!*